# Chicago Seven

## Testimony from the
## 1968 Democratic Convention
## Conspiracy Trial

Red and Black Publishers, St Petersburg, Florida

Library of Congress Cataloging-in-Publication Data

Chicago Seven : testimony from the 1968 Democratic convention conspiracy trial.
        p. cm.
    ISBN 978-1-934941-35-5
1. Chicago Seven Trial, Chicago, Ill., 1969-1970. 2. Trials (Conspiracy)--Illinois--
Chicago. I. Red and Black Publishers (Firm)
    KF224.D37C45 2008
    345.773'1102--dc22

                                                                        2008023500

Red and Black Publishers, PO Box 7542, St Petersburg, Florida, 33734
Contact us at: info@RedandBlackPublishers.com

Printed and manufactured in the United States of America

# Contents

# *Introduction*

## Stage and Cast: A Short History of the 60's

The 1960's were a unique period in American history. For a period of ten years, to a degree never seen before or since, the entire structure of American society was examined critically by a new generation, and was found to be wanting in nearly every aspect. Protest, dissent and civil disobedience were everywhere; talk of revolution was not only commonplace, but was seriously listened to, advocated and debated. No area of authority or social convention was left unchallenged — the movement against the Vietnam War questioned the post-World War II American role in the world and its ideological justifications; the flowering of Asian religious traditions challenged the authority of the mainstream American churches; the hippie culture of drugs, free love, "flower power" and individualism challenged conventional morality; the civil rights, gay rights and women's rights movements unraveled and re-wrote existing race relations, gender roles and sexual relationships; the environmental movement attacked industrialization and its effects; the "New Left" challenged the very basis of the "free market" economy and faceless bureaucratic authority; and a series of demonstrations, protest rallies, sit-ins, teach-ins, and other actions, legal and illegal, challenged conventional "law and order" and undermined all of the traditional authority structures. Political figures from both the Democratic and Republican Parties became the targets of wrath, as activists for social justice came to reject both traditional parties in favor of "direct action" and "democracy in the streets". The "generation gap" grew into a yawning chasm, as young people across the US smoked dope, listened to "acid rock", read Marcuse and Sartre, and tried to change the entire world that their parents had lived in. "Don't trust anyone over thirty", they declared.

The "Establishment", in turn, looked on, stupefied and mystified. It had never faced anything like this before, and did not know how to deal with the onslaught, and in the end it turned to the only effective weapon it had – pure repression. Under both the Democratic administration of Lyndon B Johnson and, after Johnson was driven from the White House, the Republican administration of Richard M Nixon, "counter-culture" activists became the target of repressive illegal programs, known as "Counter-Intelligence Programs", or "COINTELPRO", by the FBI, CIA, NSA and IRS to disrupt, harass, spy on and "neutralize" dissidents and political opponents. Phones were illegally tapped, mail was illegally intercepted, and provocateurs were used to drum up bogus criminal charges that were used to attempt to remove activists, like Martin Luther King Jr, Cesar Chavez, John Lennon, and others, from political action.

The iconic episode of the "generation gap" took place in Chicago in 1969. An assortment of eight (later reduced to seven) political activists were charged in Federal Court with criminal conspiracy to disrupt the 1968 Democratic Party Convention in Chicago. On one side, stood The Establishment –

the judge, the prosecuting attorneys, the police, the political officials, all declaring that they were acting to defend "law and order", to "preserve the peace" and to "protect the authority of the US Government". On the other side, stood The Movement – civil rights militants, New Left radicals, hippie music-and-drug gurus, and anti-war protestors, all declaring that they were acting to promote "grassroots democracy", to give "power to the people", and to "change America". Facing each other in court, the two sides re-enacted, in microcosm, the social and political battle that had already been raging for years in the streets. And, just as the national political and social conflicts that produced it, the courtroom trial became part sermon, part theater, part comic relief, part law and order, part repression, and part media event.

## The Civil Rights Movement

In terms of its impact on American society, perhaps the most important social movement of the 60's was the African-American movement for civil rights.

Theoretically, the American Civil War resulted in the end of slavery and the establishment of Black Americans as full citizens with all the rights of citizenship. In reality, though, this didn't happen. When Reconstruction ended, the South came under the control of a virtual single-party political machine, in which Southern Democrats (known as "Dixiecrats"), dominated the Federal and state offices, and within a few decades had implemented a maze of laws and restrictions that turned the South into an apartheid system of racial segregation, known as "Jim Crow", which left African-Americans voteless, powerless and rightless. By law, Black Americans could not go to the same schools, drink from the same water fountains, eat at the same restaurants, or swim in the same pools as whites. They could not even sit in the front seats of city buses. "Poll taxes" and other "voting requirements", meanwhile, insured that African-Americans could not vote, and not a single Black was elected to any political office. The Jim Crow system lasted from the 1890's to the 1950's, virtually unchanged and unchallenged.

The first crack in Jim Crow came in 1954. The National Association for the Advancement of Colored People (NAACP), formed in 1909 to win equal rights for African-Americans through litigation and political lobbying, filed suit in Arkansas against segregated schools. In the landmark *Brown v Board of Education* case, the Supreme Court agreed that segregated schools were a violation of the Constitution, and ordered that all public schools be made racially integrated.

Southern racist political authorities, however, openly defied the Court decision. White supremacist groups like the Ku Klux Klan and the White Citizens Councils used terrorism and fear to oppose integration, and on several occasions, the Federal government had to order US Army troops in to maintain order and enforce the law.

To counter this resistance, African-American activists decided on a course of "civil disobedience" and "nonviolent resistance", in which boycotts, sit-ins, mass rallies and other actions would be used to force an end to segregation much more quickly and certainly than legal lawsuits and lobbying could.

One of the earliest successes of the civil rights movement was a boycott in Montgomery, Alabama. In 1955, after Rosa Parks was arrested for refusing to give up her bus seat to a white person, a boycott of the city bus system was organized by local preacher Martin Luther King Jr. After a year, a Federal Court ordered Montgomery to desegregate its mass transit system. With this success, King joined with other civil rights activists to form the Southern Christian Leadership Conference (SCLC), which practiced Gandhian nonviolence as a strategy to force social change.

In 1960, four African-American students sat down at a segregated lunch counter at a Woolworth's store in Greensboro, North Carolina, and refused to leave until they were served. The sit-in sparked worldwide attention, and soon "sit-ins" were being organized at segregated facilities across the country. By the end of the year, student activists formed the Student Nonviolent Coordinating Committee (SNCC – pronounced "snick") to continue and expand the fight. In 1961, SNCC began organizing "Freedom Rides", in which African-American and white civil rights workers piled into buses to desegregate Southern bus terminals, water fountains, and other public facilities. White supremacists responded by beating the activists, often with the cooperation of local law enforcement officials. "Freedom" buses were sometimes firebombed or shot at, and several "freedom riders" were killed.

SCLC, under the leadership of Martin Luther King, and SNCC soon began to cooperate on larger campaigns. During a desegregation campaign in Birmingham, Alabama, in 1963, police commissioner "Bull" Connor unleashed fire hoses and attack dogs on the marchers. King was arrested and, in his cell, wrote "Letter From a Birmingham Jail", spelling out the goals of the civil rights movement.

In 1963, King, SCLC and SNCC organized the March on Washington, and King's address to the 250,000 marchers, "I Have a Dream", became one of the most famous speeches in American history.

In the wake of the March on Washington, the 1964 Civil Rights Act was passed by Congress. In the South, however, local Dixiecrat politicians still refused to follow the law, and in response, the civil rights movement organized Freedom Summer, a massive effort to register Black voters and challenge racist institutions across the South. Three civil rights workers, two of them white students from the North, were murdered by the Klan.

Despite the 1964 civil rights law, the elections in Southern states were still heavily rigged by the racist Dixiecrats. When the Mississippi Democratic Party "elected" an all-white slate of delegates to the Democratic Party Convention in Atlantic City, New Jersey, civil rights groups organized a "counter-election" and chose a "Mississippi Freedom Democratic Party" slate instead. The Democratic Party had expected the Convention to be a celebration of Lyndon Johnson's bold actions on behalf of civil rights; instead, the Convention got a firsthand look at the racism in its own ranks. The Mississippi Freedom slate went directly to the Credentials Committee in an effort to be seated at the Convention instead of the all-white official delegation. In response, other Southern states threatened to withdraw their own (all-white) delegations from the Convention if any of the African-Americans were seated. The Freedom slate was denied credentials, but after most of the official Mississippi delegates walked out in protest of the Party's civil rights actions, the Freedom delegates were given passes by sympathetic delegates and sat in the vacant seats, singing civil rights anthems. The next day, when the empty seats disappeared, they stood in the aisles and continued singing.

The Freedom Summer campaign (and the embarrassment caused to the Democratic Party by the Mississippi Freedom delegates) led to the 1965 Voting Right Act, which repealed all of the Jim Crow-era impediments to Black voters, and used the resources of the Federal Government to enforce voting rights.

In 1968, Martin Luther King Jr was shot and killed in Memphis, Tennessee. Even before his death, however, a faction had appeared in the civil rights movement that rejected King's reliance on nonviolence, and, impatient with the slow progress being made through legal actions and political maneuvering, advocated that "Black Power" be brought to bear on white racism.

# Black Power

Martin Luther King and the Southern Christian Leadership Conference based their strategy on two ideas; the idea that nonviolent civil disobedience, in the tradition of Thoreau and Gandhi, was the only method that the civil rights movement should use, and the idea that white liberal supporters were encouraged to join the movement as friends and advisors.

In the early 60's, the best-known critic of both of those propositions was Malcolm X, who was a spokesman for the Nation of Islam. Rather than adherence to nonviolence, Malcolm X declared that African-Americans should win their rights "by any means necessary", and advised Blacks to own and carry guns to defend themselves from white racists. Malcolm also argued that the organization of Blacks for civil rights was something that Blacks had to do for themselves – he encouraged white supporters to work against racism in their own communities, but insisted that they should play no leadership role within the African-American civil rights movement.

In 1966, in the face of massive and violent resistance to the Freedom Riders and Freedom Summer, a faction within the Student Nonviolent Coordinating Committee began to echo Malcolm X's call. When Stokely Carmichael assumed leadership of SNCC, he called for Black activists to arm themselves as a method of defense against the Klan and other racist attacks. Carmichael also made the first calls for "Black Power". After expelling whites from leadership positions within SNCC, Carmichael pointedly changed the name of the organization from the Student *Nonviolent* Coordinating Committee to the Student *National* Coordinating Committee. The calls for "Black Power" and "Black Pride" (and the rejection of the racist term "Negro") led to a renaissance of African culture in America, with Black activists taking up the study of the Swahili language and African clothing and hairstyles.

When Martin Luther King was assassinated in 1968, Stokely Carmichael remarked that the white racists had killed the one man who could control Black anger, and that every major city in the US would now burn to the ground.

# Black Panther Party

The organization that, above all, personified the idea of Black Power, was the Black Panther Party.

In 1965, the Watts section of Los Angeles, frustrated by years of white racism and brutality at the hands of white police, exploded in riot. A year later, Huey P Newton and Bobby G Seale, inspired by Stokely Carmichael's call for Black Power, formed an organization they called the Black Panther Party for Self-Defense. Carmichael soon became a member, as did activists Fred Hampton and Eldridge Cleaver.

The Black Panther Party took its inspiration from two sources. From the speeches of Malcolm X, came the program of black nationalism, armed self-defense, and Black Power. From the writings of Marx and Lenin, came an internationalist and socialist program that viewed African-Americans as part of an "underclass" that was being forced into a revolutionary attitude by its repressed social position. Along with "Black Power", the Panthers declared "Power to the People".

The Panthers organized a series of community services in Black neighborhoods, including free medical clinics, drug and alcohol rehabilitation programs, and free breakfasts for school children. Much of the Panther activity, however, focused on self-defense against police brutality. In 1966, fewer than 20 of Oakland's 660 police officers were African-American, and the white police had reputations as racist bullies. To combat police brutality, the Panthers sent armed patrols to follow the police and to intervene if necessary to protect civil rights. When the state of California tried to pass a law making it illegal to openly carry loaded weapons, the Panthers marched on the state capitol, openly carrying their loaded shotguns. Armed police and armed Panthers clashed on many occasions, with deaths resulting on both sides. On one occasion, Panther organizer Fred Hampton was shot, unarmed in bed, during a police raid

The Black Panther Party, with its militant Black Power stance and its open display of firearms, scared the hell out of white Establishment America, and was a primary target for the FBI's illegal COINTELPRO program. And, with its Marxist-Leninist rhetoric, the Panthers soon became the darlings of another revolutionary social movement, one that called itself "The New Left".

# The New Left

By the 1960's, it was apparent that the Marxism of the oldline Communist Parties was dead. The Soviet Union had descended into dictatorship, the militant labor movements of the 30's were gone, and uprisings in Czechoslovakia, Poland, and Hungary had loosened the USSR's ideological grip on the world communist movement. Radicals in the US, therefore, began to call for a New Left, one based not on authoritarian central authority, but on decentralized grassroots democracy. They were heavily influenced by syndicalist and anarchist ideas.

The organization that took up the call for a New Left began as the student wing of the old-school socialist group League for Industrial Democracy. In 1960, the Student League for Industrial Democracy broke with its parent organization, embraced a New Left viewpoint, and changed its name to Students for a Democratic Society (SDS). In 1962, SDS member Tom Hayden wrote the group's call for revolution, known as the Port Huron Statement. The Port Huron Statement called for "participatory democracy", in which grassroots political organization would be the weapon to bring about an end to the nuclear arms race, racial discrimination, poverty, and corporate domination. Hayden became President of the new organization.

For several years, SDS existed only as a small socialist education society with chapters in a few universities and colleges. One of these was the University of California at Berkeley. In October 1964, the campus administration attempted to close down the makeshift booths that SDS and other student political groups used to distribute literature on campus. In response, the Free Speech Movement virtually shut down the Berkeley campus with sit-ins and protests, until students were once again given the right to set up literature booths on campus.

When President Lyndon Johnson escalated the Vietnam War in 1965 by bombing North Vietnam, and began expanding the draft to support the war, SDS chapters on several campuses responded by organizing local protest rallies. SDS organized "teach-ins", in which organizers explained to large groups of students what the war was all about and how they could organize to oppose it. By 1966, SDS was the largest student antiwar organization in the US. Embraced by the Black Panther Party, the New Left in turn became increasingly more militant in its Marxist and socialist rhetoric.

In the spring of 1968, SDS called for "Days of Resistance" against the Vietnam War, and local chapters responded with teach-ins, sit-ins, rallies and a national student strike on April 26.

# The Anti-War Movement

In 1954, the French, after losing a battle at Dien Bien Phu to an insurgent army led by Communist Ho Chi Minh, withdrew from their colony in Vietnam. An international conference in Geneva was called to decide what to do with Vietnam, and it was decided that the country would be temporarily divided in two, with the northern section under Ho's rule and the southern under the leadership of Ngo Din Diem. Elections were to be held in 1956 to reunify the country. Diem, however, refused to hold any elections and assumed power on his own. The US, meanwhile, refused to sign the Geneva accords and began giving military assistance to the Diem government. Diem's brutally heavy-handed methods, however, alienated most Vietnamese, and he was overthrown in 1963 in a US-backed coup. South Vietnam was then run by a series of military governments.

In 1964, two American destroyers in Vietnamese waters reported (wrongly) that they had been fired upon by North Vietnamese gunboats. As a result, Congress passed the Gulf of Tonkin Resolution giving President Johnson authority to carry out military actions in Vietnam. By 1968, there were 200,000 American troops in Vietnam, and the Tet Offensive demonstrated that they were no closer to "victory" than they had been in 1964. As the number of young people who were being drafted (some 40,000 people per month) and sent to Vietnam continued to climb, opposition to the war increased, particularly when it seemed that the war was essentially a political one, and the escalating military involvement was accomplishing nothing. TV images of the war showed massive Vietnamese civilian casualties. Antiwar sentiment increased, and antiwar rallies in Washington DC routinely attracted 250,000 people. The war turned into a political disaster for President Lyndon Johnson – antiwar protestors outside the White House chanted "Hey, hey, LBJ—how many kids did you kill today?" Johnson, for his part, believed that "foreign powers" were behind the antiwar movement, and directed many of the FBI's illegal COINTELPRO efforts against various antiwar organizations, including Vietnam Veterans Against the War.

In the 1968 Presidential campaign, Senator Eugene McCarthy ran against Johnson in the Democratic primaries on an antiwar platform, and did well. As Johnson's popularity declined, he surprised the nation by announcing that he would not run for re-election. Johnson's Vice President, Hubert Humphrey, entered the race and pledged to continue American military actions in Vietnam.

By 1967, various antiwar groups had united into a coalition called the National Mobilization Committee to End the War In Vietnam, more commonly known as "The Mobe". In October 1967, the Mobe organized a march on the Pentagon with 100,000 people. Some 800 protestors were arrested at the Pentagon for civil disobedience. Among the most theatrical and flamboyant protestors were the "Youth International Party", more widely known as "The Yippies".

# The Yippies

The Yippies had their beginnings in the hippie counter-culture. The hippies (no one is quite sure where the name came from) first came to life in the Haight-Ashbury district of San Francisco, where a group of young people, many of them veterans of the Berkeley Free Speech Movement, adopted a lifestyle that emphasized peace, love, and individual freedom. The wide-ranging hippie philosophy borrowed heavily from Eastern philosophy and Native American traditions, and they often referred to themselves as a "tribe". The hippies rejected Establishment values and embraced free sexuality, individual liberation, ecological awareness, and the use of drugs like marijuana and LSD to expand consciousness. Many hippies lived in large communes where everything was shared equally, rejecting the American culture of materialism and greed. They also rejected the American sense of aesthetics, which they viewed as a faceless mass of grey colorless "organization men", and their clothing and art displayed an explosion of color – tie-dyed t-shirts, long hair, beaded jewelry, flowers, and colorful headbands became the hippie dress of choice.

In early 1967, a series of "be-ins" were held in San Francisco and New York, where thousands of beaded and bearded young people gathered to simply "be", and to "celebrate the beauty of the universe and the beauty of being".

While the hippies viewed themselves as a counter culture and a deliberate challenge to mainstream American society, most of them rejected any sort of organized political action, dismissing it as a "power trip". One outgrowth of the hippie movement, however, not only advocated direct political action, but viewed the hippie counter-culture as a vehicle for doing it.

Without doubt, the Yippies were the most unique political movement ever experienced in American history.

The Yippies were never a real organization; there was never any formal organization or membership. They never even had a real name; although they sometimes used the mocking title "Youth International Party" (a name used by no one, except the utterly humorless FBI), the name was simply a play on "yip yip yippeeee!", the cry of the Native American coyote trickster.

The most prominent "spokesmen" for the Yippie movement were Jerry Rubin and Abbie Hoffman. In their speeches and writings, they advocated a "New Nation" that was based on the hippie ethic of peace, love, and individual freedom. "We are a people," one Yippie leaflet declared. "We are a New Nation. We want everyone to control their own life and to care for one another."

Rejecting the tired old authoritarian politics of the Old Left (one Yippie declared that if the oldline Left ever gained power, the first thing they would do is force the hippies to shave and get a haircut), the Yippies embarked on a program to topple American culture by making fun of it. Understanding the power of mass media, and with an uncanny eye for street theater and symbolic imagery, the Yippies used pranks, put-ons and "guerrilla theater" to mock the Establishment and point out its absurdities. In one famous incident, a group of Yippies took a guided tour of the New York Stock Exchange, and when the tour reached a balcony overlooking the trading floor, they threw hundreds of dollar bills over the railing. The entire stock exchange shut down, as visitors were treated to the sight of wealthy white stocktraders in three-piece suits madly scrambling over top of each other to grab as many dollar bills as they could. In another piece of theater, when Jerry Rubin was subpeonaed to testify before the House Un-American Activities Committee, he appeared dressed in the uniform of a Revolutionary War soldier, passing out copies of the Declaration of Independence to onlookers.

In 1967, the Yippies organized a massive rally at the Pentagon to protest the Vietnam War. With typical humor, they announced that they intended to invite a group of witches to exorcise the Pentagon of its evil spirits, and calmly applied for a permit to "levitate the entire building". A newspaper photograph at the event, showing beaded hippies placing flowers into the rifle barrels of National Guard troops, became an iconic image of the 1960's.

To the Yippie pranksters, the upcoming Democratic Convention was a golden opportunity for deviltry and theatrics on a mass scale.

# The Chicago Demonstrations

After the assassination of Robert Kennedy, who was running on an antiwar platform, in June 1968, it became apparent that Vice President Hubert Humphrey would be the Democratic nominee, and that he would continue the unpopular war in Vietnam.

In response, counter-culture groups began to discuss plans to protest at the site of the Convention, in Chicago. The national coordinator for the National Mobilization to End the War in Vietnam (The Mobe), Rennie Davis, declared that "there are thousands of young people in this country who do not want to see a rigged convention rubber-stamp another four years of Lyndon Johnson's war". In March 1968, representatives of several antiwar groups, including The Mobe's Rennie Davis and Tom Hayden, antiwar activist David Dellinger, and Yippies Jerry Rubin and Abbie Hoffman, met near Chicago to organize demonstrations at the convention. The Yippies had already issued their own call for "A Festival of Life" at the Convention. In typical exuberant Yippie style, they declared:

> "Join us in Chicago in August for an international festival of youth, music, and theater. Rise up and abandon the creeping meatball! Come all you rebels, youth spirits, rock minstrels, truth-seekers, peacock-freaks, poets, barricade-jumpers, dancers, lovers and artists!
>
> "It is summer. It is the last week in August, and the NATIONAL DEATH PARTY meets to bless Lyndon Johnson. We are there! There are 50,000 of us dancing in the streets, throbbing with amplifiers and harmony. We are making love in the parks. We are reading, singing, laughing, printing newspapers, groping, and making a mock convention, and celebrating the birth of FREE AMERICA in our own time.
>
> "Everything will be free. Bring blankets, tents, draft-cards, body-paint, Mr. Leary's Cow, food to share,

music, eager skin, and happiness. The threats of LBJ, Mayor Daley, and J. Edgar Freako will not stop us. We are coming! We are coming from all over the world!

"The life of the American spirit is being torn asunder by the forces of violence, decay, and the napalm-cancer fiend. We demand the Politics of Ecstasy! We are the delicate spores of the new fierceness that will change America. We will create our own reality, we are Free America! And we will not accept the false theater of the Death Convention.

"We will be in Chicago. Begin preparations now! Chicago is yours! Do it!"

The Mobe planned a series of teach-ins and mass demonstrations. The Yippies, more creatively (and far less seriously), announced fanciful plans for a public "fuck-in", declared that they would slip LSD into the city's water supply, would infiltrate the Convention by seducing the delegates' wives and daughters, and would pull down Hubert Humphrey's pants while he spoke at the podium. They also proposed to nominate a pig (named "Pigasus The Immortal") as the Democratic Party's presidential candidate.

The Establishment confronted The Movement in the form of Mayor Richard Daley, who ran Chicago like a virtual fiefdom. When the demonstrators asked for a permit to sleep in the city parks, Daley denied the request and announced that an 11 pm curfew would be enforced. After an appeal to a Federal court failed to overturn the curfew, several protest groups called off the planned demonstration, but many protestors were already in Chicago. With nowhere else to go, they stayed in the park until curfew, when the Chicago police waded in each night with batons swinging, indiscriminately clubbing protestors, journalists, and passers-by, in what was later officially called "a police riot". TV cameras showed images of helmeted police beating young people into unconsciousness, while the onlooking crowd chanted "The whole world is watching". Inside the convention, outraged delegate Senator Abraham

Ribicoff took to the podium to denounce the "Gestapo tactics being used in the city of Chicago".

# The Trial

In the wake of the Chicago riots, LBJ's Attorney General, Ramsey Clark, began preparing to prosecute the Chicago police who had brutalized demonstrators and onlookers. After the Richard Nixon Adminstration took office in 1969, however, the priorities were reversed, and Attorney General John Mitchell gave the order to prosecute the "conspirators" who had organized the demonstrations. Eight people were subsequently indicted for crossing interstate lines for the purpose of organizing a riot. They were Abbie Hoffman and Jerry Rubin of the Yippies, Tom Hayden and Rennie Davis of the Mobe, David Dellinger of the Catholic antiwar movement, Bobby Seale of the Black Panther Party, sociology professor Lee Weiner (who was charged with conspiring to make Molotov cocktails for use in the riots), and chemist John Froines (who was charged with conspiring to make "stink bombs" for use against the police). The trial of the "Chicago Eight" began in September 1969.

The judge in the case was Julius Hoffman, a middle-aged conservative man who was utterly unprepared for the circus that was about to invade his courtroom.

The tone for the trial was set right from the beginning. Defense attorneys William Kunstler and Leonard Weinglass submitted a list of 54 questions that they wanted to ask of potential jurors, including "Would you let your daughter marry a Yippie?" and "Do you know who Janis Joplin or Jimi Hendrix is?" The judge rejected all these questions but one, agreeing only to ask jurors if they had any relatives or friends who worked in law enforcement.

Despite the accusations of "conspiracy", the eight defendants were in fact widely different in demeanor, tactics, and political goals. "Conspiracy?" snorted Abbie Hoffman. "Hell, we couldn't agree on lunch." Some of the defendants, led by Tom Hayden, wanted to take the trial at face value, and present a reasoned defense based upon gaping holes in the prosecution's case (most of the "conspirators" had never even met each other before the trial began). Rubin and Hoffman, by contrast, wanted to turn the whole trial into "political theater".

Bobby Seale, meanwhile, was fighting to get a lawyer for the trial. His own attorney was in the hospital recuperating from gallbladder surgery, and Seale made a motion to delay the trial until his own attorney could represent him or, failing that, to be allowed to represent himself until then. The judge summarily rejected both requests and, when Seale loudly insisted on his right to counsel of choice, had the defendant gagged and handcuffed to his chair. For several days, the world press saw the powerful image of a black man in America literally bound and gagged by white American justice. After several days, the judge removed Seale from the case, to give him a separate trial later. The "Chicago Eight" now became the "Chicago Seven".

The prosecutors, Thomas Foran and Richard Schultz, based their conspiracy case on written statements made by the defendants before the rallies, and through the testimony of a series of police informants who had infiltrated the Yippies, SDS and the Mobe.

The defendants, who lounged around the courtroom table in blue jeans and colorful t-shirts, turned the trial into a circus and a platform for counter-culture ideas. A long string of witnesses, from writer Norman Mailer to LSD guru Timothy Leary to singer Phil Ochs, were called to testify about the hippie culture, the New Left, and the Vietnam War. The judge refused to allow the jury to hear any of it. Only three of the defendants testified – Hoffman, Davis and Seale, and Seale's testimony was not heard by the jury either. The judge consistently ruled against the defendants on all substantive questions (documents later revealed that the FBI had illegally bugged the defense attorneys and were listening in on all their strategy sessions, with the knowledge and support of the judge), prompting the frustrated defense attorneys to frequent outbursts that led to almost 160 contempt of court charges. Abbie Hoffman and Jerry Rubin amused themselves by blowing kisses to the jury, by showing up in court dressed in judicial robes, and by displaying the Viet Cong flag on the table.

The jury acquitted everyone of the conspiracy charge, but convicted five of the defendants on charges of crossing a state line to incite a riot. Froines and Weiner were both acquitted of charges of making bombs. The judge sentenced each of the five convicted defendants to five years in jail and a $5,000 fine, and sentenced the two defense attorneys to multi-year terms for contempt of court. After the trial, one juror told the newspaper that he thought all the defendants should have been convicted just because of their appearance, while another juror remarked that she wished the Chicago police had just shot them all.

Two years later, the appeals court, citing the judge's "antagonistic attitude towards the defense" and "the wrongdoing of FBI agents", reversed all the convictions and dropped all the charges.

# Testimony Of Abbie Hoffman

MR. WEINGLASS: Will you please identify yourself for the record?

THE WITNESS: My name is Abbie. I am an orphan of America.

MR. SCHULTZ: Your Honor, may the record show it is the defendant Hoffman who has taken the stand?

THE COURT: Oh, yes. It may so indicate. . . .

MR. WEINGLASS: Where do you reside?

THE WITNESS: I live in Woodstock Nation.

MR. WEINGLASS: Will you tell the Court and jury where it is?

THE WITNESS: Yes. It is a nation of alienated young people. We carry it around with us as a state of mind in the same way as the Sioux Indians carried the Sioux nation around with them. It is a nation dedicated to cooperation versus competition, to the idea that people should have better means of exchange than property or money, that there should be some other basis for human interaction. It is a nation dedicated to—

THE COURT: Just where it is, that is all.

THE WITNESS: It is in my mind and in the minds of my brothers and sisters. It does not consist of property or material but, rather, of ideas and certain values. We believe in a society —

THE COURT: No, we want the place of residence, if he has one, place of doing business, if you have a business. Nothing about philosophy or India, sir. Just where you live, if you have a place to live. Now you said Woodstock. In what state is Woodstock?

THE WITNESS: It is in the state of mind, in the mind of myself and my brothers and sisters. It is a conspiracy. Presently, the nation is held captive, in the penitentiaries of the institutions of a decaying system.

MR. WEINGLASS: Can you tell the Court and jury your present age?

THE WITNESS: My age is 33. I am a child of the 60s.

MR. WEINGLASS: When were you born?

THE WITNESS: Psychologically, 1960.

MR. SCHULTZ: Objection, if the Court please. I move to strike the answer.

MR. WEINGLASS: What is the actual date of your birth?

THE WITNESS: November 30, 1936.

MR. WEINGLASS: Between the date of your birth, November 30, 1936, and May 1, 1960, what if anything occurred in your life?

THE WITNESS: Nothing. I believe it is called an American education.

MR. SCHULTZ: Objection.

THE COURT: I sustain the objection.

THE WITNESS: Huh.

MR. WEINGLASS: Abbie, could you tell the Court and jury —

MR. SCHULTZ: His name isn't Abbie. I object to this informality.

MR. WEINGLASS: Can you tell the Court and jury what is your present occupation?

---

THE WITNESS: I am a cultural revolutionary. Well, I am really a defendant — full-time.

MR. WEINGLASS: What do you mean by the phrase "cultural revolutionary?"

THE WITNESS: Well, I suppose it is a person who tries to shape and participate in the values, and the mores, the customs and the style of living of new people who eventually become inhabitants of a new nation and a new society through art and poetry, theater, and music.

MR. WEINGLASS: What have you done yourself to participate in that revolution?

THE WITNESS: Well, I have been a rock and roll singer. I am a reporter with the Liberation News Service. I am a poet. I am a film maker. I made a movie called "Yippies Tour Chicago or How I Spent My Summer Vacation." Currently, I am negotiating with United Artists and MGM to do a movie in Hollywood.

I have written an extensive pamphlet on how to live free in the city of New York.

I have written two books, one called *Revolution for The Hell of It* under the pseudonym Free, and one called, *Woodstock Nation.*

MR. WEINGLASS: Taking you back to the spring of 1960, approximately May 1, 1960, will you tell the Court and jury where you were?

MR. SCHULTZ: 1960?

THE WITNESS: That's right.

MR. SCHULTZ: Objection.

THE COURT: I sustain the objection.

MR. WEINGLASS: Your Honor, that date has great relevance to the trial. May 1, 1960, was this witness' first public demonstration. I am going to bring him down through Chicago.

THE COURT: Not in my presence, you are not going to bring him down. I sustain the objection to the question.

THE WITNESS: My background has nothing to do with my state of mind?

THE COURT: Will you remain quiet while I am making a ruling? I know you have no respect for me.

MR. KUNSTLER: Your Honor, that is totally unwarranted. I think your remarks call for a motion for a mistrial.

THE COURT: And your motion calls for a denial of the motion. Mr. Weinglass, continue with your examination.

MR. KUNSTLER: You denied my motion? I hadn't even started to argue it.

THE COURT: I don't need any argument on that one. The witness turned his back on me while he was on the witness stand.

THE WITNESS: I was just looking at the pictures of the long hairs up on the wall . . . .

THE COURT: . . . . I will let the witness tell about this asserted conversation with Mr. Rubin on the occasion described.

MR. WEINGLASS: What was the conversation at that time?

THE WITNESS: Jerry Rubin told me that he had come to New York to be project director of a peace march in Washington that was going to march to the Pentagon in October, October 21. He said that the peace movement suffered from a certain kind of attitude, mainly that it was based solely on the issue of the Vietnam war. He said that the war in Vietnam was not just an accident but a direct by-product of the kind of system, a capitalist system in the country, and that we had to begin to put forth new kinds of values, especially to young people in the country, to make a kind of society in which a Vietnam war would not be possible.

And he felt that these attitudes and values were present in the hippie movement and many of the techniques, the guerrilla theater techniques that had been used and many of these methods of communication would allow for people to participate and become involved in a new kind of democracy.

I said that the Pentagon was a five-sided evil symbol in most religions and that it might be possible to approach this from a religious point of view. If we got large numbers of people to surround the Pentagon, we could exorcize it of its evil spirits.

So I had agreed at that point to begin working on the exorcism of the Pentagon demonstration.

MR. WEINGLASS: Prior to the date of the demonstration which is October, did you go to the Pentagon?

THE WITNESS: Yes. I went about a week or two before with one of my close brothers, Martin Carey, a poster maker, and we measured the Pentagon, the two of us, to see how many people would fit around it. We only had to do one side because it is just multiplied by five.

We got arrested. It's illegal to measure the Pentagon. I didn't know it up to that point.

When we were arrested they asked us what we were doing. We said it was to measure the Pentagon and we wanted a permit to raise it 300 feet in the air, and they said "How about 10?" So we said "OK".

And they threw us out of the Pentagon and we went back to New York and had a press conference, told them what it was about.

We also introduced a drug called *lace*, which, when you squirted it at the policemen made them take their clothes off and make love, a very potent drug.

MR. WEINGLASS: Did you mean literally that the building was to rise up 300 feet off the ground?

MR. SCHULTZ: I can't cross-examine about his meaning literally.

THE COURT: I sustain the objection.

MR. SCHULTZ: I would ask Mr. Weinglass please get on with the trial of this case and stop playing around with raising the Pentagon 10 feet or 300 feet off the ground.

MR. WEINGLASS: Your Honor, I am glad to see Mr. Schultz finally concedes that things like levitating the Pentagon building, putting LSD in the water, 10,000 people walking nude on Lake Michigan, and a $200,000 bribe attempt are all playing around. I am willing to concede that fact, that it was all playing around, it was a play idea of this witness, and if he is willing to concede it, we can all go home.

THE COURT: I sustain the objection.

MR. WEINGLASS: Did you intend that the people who surrounded the Pentagon should do anything of a violent nature whatever to cause the building to rise 300 feet in the air and be exercised of evil spirits?

MR. SCHULTZ: Objection.

THE COURT: I sustain the objection.

MR. WEINGLASS: Could you indicate to the Court and jury whether or not the Pentagon was, in fact, exercised of its evil spirits?

THE WITNESS: Yes, I believe it was. . . .

MR. WEINGLASS: Now, drawing your attention to the first week of December 1967, did you have occasion to meet with Jerry Rubin and the others?

THE WITNESS: Yes.

MR. WEINGLASS: Will you relate to the Court and jury what the conversation was?

THE WITNESS: Yes.

We talked about the possibility of having demonstrations at the Democratic Convention in Chicago, Illinois, that was going to be occurring that August. I am not sure that we knew at that point that it was in Chicago. Wherever it was, we were planning on going.

Jerry Rubin, I believe, said that it would be a good idea to call it the Festival of Life in contrast to the Convention of Death, and to have it in some kind of public area, like a park or something, in Chicago.

One thing that I was very particular about was that we didn't have any concept of leadership involved. There was a feeling of young people that they didn't want to listen to leaders. We had to create a kind of situation in which people would be allowed to participate and become in a real sense their own leaders.

I think it was then after this that Paul Krassner said the word "YIPPIE," and we felt that that expressed in a kind of slogan and advertising sense the spirit that we wanted to put forth in Chicago, and we adopted that as our password, really. . . .

Anita [Hoffman] said that "Yippie" would be understood by

our generation, that straight newspapers like the *New York Times* and the U.S. Government and the courts and everything wouldn't take it seriously unless it had a formal name, so she came up with the name: "Youth International Party." She said we could play a lot of jokes on the concept of "party" because everybody would think that we were this huge international conspiracy, but that in actuality we were a party that you had fun at.

Nancy [Kursham] said that fun was an integral ingredient, that people in America, because they were being programmed like IBM cards, weren't having enough fun in life and that if you watched television, the only people that you saw having any fun were people who were buying lousy junk on television commercials, and that this would be a whole new attitude because you would see people, young people, having fun while they were protesting the system, and that young people all around this country and around the world would be turned on for that kind of an attitude.

I said that fun was very important, too, that it was a direct rebuttal of the kind of ethics and morals that were being put forth in the country to keep people working in a rat race which didn't make any sense because in a few years that machines would do all the work anyway, that there was a whole system of values that people were taught to postpone their pleasure, to put all their money in the bank, to buy life insurance, a whole bunch of things that didn't make any sense to our generation at all, and that fun actually was becoming quite subversive.

Jerry said that because of our action at the Stock Exchange in throwing out the money, that within a few weeks the Wall Street brokers there had totally enclosed the whole stock exchange in bulletproof, shatterproof glass, that cost something like $20,000 because they were afraid we'd come back and throw money out again.

He said that for hundreds of years political cartoonists had always pictured corrupt politicians in the guise of a pig, and he said that it would be great theater if we ran a pig for President, and we all took that on as like a great idea and that's more or less — that was the founding.

MR. WEINGLASS: The document that is before you, D-222 for identification, what is that document?

THE WITNESS: It was our initial call to people to describe what Yippie was about and why we were coming to Chicago.

Mk. WEINGLASS: Now, Abbie, could you read the entire document to the jury.

THE WITNESS: It says:

"A STATEMENT FROM YIP!

"Join us in Chicago in August for an international festival of youth, music, and theater. Rise up and abandon the creeping meatball! Come all you rebels, youth spirits, rock minstrels, truth-seekers, peacock-freaks, poets, barricade-jumpers, dancers, lovers and artists!

"It is summer. It is the last week in August, and the NATIONAL DEATH PARTY meets to bless Lyndon Johnson. We are there! There are 50,000 of us dancing in the streets, throbbing with amplifiers and harmony. We are making love in the parks. We are reading, singing, laughing, printing newspapers, groping, and making a mock convention, and celebrating the birth of FREE AMERICA in our own time.

"Everything will be free. Bring blankets, tents, draft-cards, body-paint, Mr. Leary's Cow, food to share, music, eager skin, and happiness. The threats of LBJ, Mayor Daley, and J. Edgar Freako will not stop us. We are coming! We are coming from all over the world!

"The life of the American spirit is being torn asunder by the forces of violence, decay, and the napalm-cancer fiend. We demand the Politics of Ecstasy! We are the delicate spores of the new fierceness that will change America. We will create our own reality, we are Free America! And we will not accept the false theater of the Death Convention.

"We will be in Chicago. Begin preparations now! Chicago is yours! Do it!"

"Do it!" was a slogan like "Yippie." We use that a lot and it meant that each person that came should take on the responsibility for being his own leader—that we should, in fact, have a leaderless society.

We shortly thereafter opened an office and people worked in the office on what we call movement salaries, subsistence, thirty dollars a week. We had what the straight world would call a staff and an office although we called it an energy center and regarded ourselves as a tribe or a family.

MR. WEINGLASS: Could you explain to the Court and jury, if you know, how this staff functioned in your office?

THE WITNESS: Well, I would describe it as anarchistic. People would pick up the phone and give information and people from all over the country were now becoming interested and they would ask for more information, whether we were going to get a permit, how the people in Chicago were relating, and we would bring flyers and banners and posters. We would have large general meetings that were open to anybody who wanted to come.

MR. WEINGLASS: How many people would attend these weekly meetings?

THE WITNESS: There were about two to three hundred people there that were attending the meetings. Eventually we had to move into Union Square and hold meetings out in the public. There would be maybe three to five hundred people attending meetings. . . .

MR. WEINGLASS: Where did you go [March 23], if you can recall.

THE WITNESS: I flew to Chicago to observe a meeting being sponsored, I believe, by the National Mobilization Committee. It was held at a place called Lake Villa, I believe, about twenty miles outside of Chicago here.

MR. WEINGLASS: Do you recall how you were dressed for that meeting?

THE WITNESS: I was dressed as an Indian. I had gone to Grand Central Station as an Indian and so I just got on a plane and flew as an Indian.

MR. WEINGLASS: Now, when you flew to Chicago, were you alone?

THE WITNESS: No. Present were Jerry, myself, Paul Krassner, and Marshall Bloom, the head of this Liberation News Service.

MR. WEINGLASS: When you arrived at Lake Villa, did you have occasion to meet any of the defendants who are seated here at this table?

THE WITNESS: Yes, I met for the first time Rennie, Tom Hayden—who I had met before, and that's it, you know. . . .

MR. WEINGLASS: Was any decision reached at that meeting about coming to Chicago?

THE WITNESS: I believe that they debated for two days about whether they should come or not to Chicago. They decided to have more meetings. We said we had already made up our minds to come to Chicago and we passed out buttons and posters and said that if they were there, good, it would be a good time.

MR. WEINGLASS: Following the Lake Villa conference, do you recall where you went?

THE WITNESS: Yes. The next day, March 25, I went to the Aragon Ballroom. It was a benefit to raise money again for the Yippies but we had a meeting backstage in one of the dressing rooms with the Chicago Yippies.

MR. WEINGLASS: Do you recall what was discussed?

THE WITNESS: Yes. We drafted a permit application for the Festival to take place in Chicago. We agreed that Grant Park would be best.

MR. WEINGLASS: Directing your attention to the following morning, which was Monday morning, March 26, do you recall where you were at that morning?

THE WITNESS: We went to the Parks Department. Jerry was there, Paul, Helen Runningwater, Abe Peck, Reverend John Tuttle—there were a group of about twenty to thirty people, Yippies.

MR. WEINGLASS: Did you meet with anyone at the Park District at that time?

THE WITNESS: Yes. There were officials from the Parks Department to greet us, they took us into this office, and we presented a permit application.

MR. WEINGLASS: Did you ever receive a reply to this application?

THE WITNESS: Not to my knowledge.

MR. WEINGLASS: After your meeting with the Park District, where, if anywhere, did you go?

THE WITNESS: We held a brief press conference on the lawn in front of the Parks Department, and then we went to see Mayor Daley at City Hall. When we arrived, we were told that the mayor was indisposed and that Deputy Mayor David Stahl would see us.

MR. WEINGLASS: When you met with Deputy Mayor Stahl, what, if anything, occurred?

THE WITNESS: Helen Runningwater presented him with a copy of the permit application that we had submitted to the Parks Department. It was rolled up in the Playmate of the Month that said "To Dick with Love, the Yippies," on it. And we presented it to him and gave him a kiss and put a Yippie button on him, and when he opened it up, the Playmate was just there.

And he was very embarrassed by the whole thing, and he said that we had followed the right procedure, the city would give it proper attention and things like that . . . .


December 29, 1969

MR. WEINGLASS: I direct your attention now to August 5, 1968, and I ask you where you were on that day.

THE WITNESS: I was in my apartment, St. Marks Place, on the Lower East Side in New York City.

MR. WEINGLASS: Who was with you?

THE WITNESS: Jerry Rubin was there, Paul Krassner was there, and Nancy. Anita was there; five of us, I believe.

MR. WEINGLASS: Can you describe the conversation which occurred between you and Abe Peck on the telephone?

THE WITNESS: Mr. Peck and other people from Chicago, Yippies—had just returned from a meeting on Monday afternoon with David Stahl and other people from the City administration. He said that he was quite shocked because—they said that they didn't know that we wanted to sleep in the park.

Abe Peck said that it had been known all along that one of the key elements of this Festival was to let us sleep in the park, that it was impossible for people to sleep in hotels since the delegates were staying there and it would only be natural to sleep in the park.

He furthermore told me in his opinion the City was laying down certain threats to them in order to try and get them to withdraw their permit application, and that we should come immediately back to Chicago.

MR. WEINGLASS: After that phone conversation what occurred?

THE WITNESS: We subsequently went to Chicago on August 7 at night.

MR.WEINGLASS: Did a meeting occur on that evening?

THE WITNESS: Yes, in Mayor Daley's press conference room, where he holds his press conferences.

MR. WEINGLASS: Can you relate what occurred at this meeting?

THE WITNESS: It was more or less an informal kind of meeting. Mr. Stahl made clear that these were just exploratory talks, that the mayor didn't have it in his power to grant the permits. We said that that was absurd, that we had been negotiating now for a period of four or five months, that the City was acting like an ostrich, sticking its head in the sand, hoping that we would all go away like it was some bad dream.

I pointed out that it was in the best interests of the City to have us in Lincoln Park ten miles away from the Convention hall. I said we had no intention of marching on the Convention hall, that I didn't particularly think that politics in America could be changed by marches and rallies, that what we were presenting was an alternative life style, and we hoped that people of Chicago would come up, and mingle in Lincoln Park and see what we were about.

I said that the City ought to give us a hundred grand, a hundred thousand dollars to run the Festival. It would be so much in their best interests.

And then I said, "Why don't you just give two hundred grand, and I'll split town?"

It was a very informal meeting. We were just sitting around on metal chairs that they had.

All the time David Stahl had been insisting that they did not make decisions in the city, that he and the mayor did not make the decisions. We greeted this with a lot of laughter and said that it was generally understood all around the country that Daley was the boss of Chicago and made all the decisions.

I also said that I considered that our right to assemble in Lincoln Park and to present our society was a right that I was willing to die for, that this was a fundamental human right . . . .

MR. WEINGLASS: On August 14, approximately three days later, in the morning of that day, do you recall where you were?

THE WITNESS: I went to speak to Jay Miller, head of the American Civil Liberties Union. I asked if it was possible for them to work with us on an injunction in the Federal court to sue Mayor Daley and other city officials about the fact that they would not grant us a permit and were denying us our right to freedom of speech and assembly.

MR. WEINGLASS: Now, can you relate to the Court and jury what happened in court when you appeared at 10:00 A.M.?

THE WITNESS: It was heard before Judge Lynch. There was a fantastic amount of guards all over the place.

We were searched, made to take off our shirts, empty our pockets —

MR. SCHULTZ. That is totally irrelevant. There happened to be threats at that time, your Honor —

THE WITNESS: He is right. There were threats. I had twenty that week.

THE COURT: The language, "There were a fantastic amount of guards," may go out and the jury is directed to disregard them.

MR. WEINGLASS: After the—

THE WITNESS: We came before the judge. It was a room similar to this, similar, kind of wall-to wall bourgeois, rugs and neon lights. Federal courts are all the same, I think. The judge made a couple of references to us in the room, said that our dress was an affront to the Court. It was pointed out by a lawyer that came by that Judge Lynch was Mayor Daley's ex-law partner. As a result of this conversation we went back into court about twenty, thirty minutes later.

MR. WEINGLASS: Did you speak to the Court?

THE WITNESS: I spoke to Judge Lynch. I said that we were withdrawing our suit, that we had as little faith in the judicial system in this country as we had in the political system.

He said, "Be careful, young man. I will find a place for you to sleep."

And I thanked him for that, said I had one, and left.

We withdrew our suit. Then we had a press conference downstairs to explain the reasons for that. We explained to the press that we were leaving in our permit application but withdrawing our Federal injunction to sue the city. We said it was a bit futile to end up before a judge, Judge Lynch, who was the ex-law partner of Mayor Daley, that the Federal judges were closely tied in with the Daley and Democratic political machine in Chicago and that we could have little recourse of grievance.

Furthermore, that we suspected that the judge would order us not to go into Lincoln Park at all and that if we did, that we would be in violation of contempt of court, and that it was a setup, and Judge Lynch planned to lynch us in the same way that Stahl was stalling us.

I pointed out that the names in this thing were getting really absurd, similarities. I also read a list of Yippie demands that I had written that morning—sort of Yippie philosophy.

MR. WEINGLASS: Now, will you read for the Court and jury the eighteen demands first, then the postscript.

THE WITNESS: I will read it in the order that I wrote it. "Revolution toward a free society, Yippie, by A. Yippie.

"This is a personal statement. There are no spokesmen for the Yippies. We are all our own leaders. We realize this list of demands is inconsistent. They are not really demands. For people to make demands of the Democratic Party is an exercise in wasted wish fulfillment. If we have a demand, it is simply and emphatically that they, along with their fellow inmates in the Republican Party, cease to exist. We demand a society built along the alternative community in Lincoln Park, a society based on humanitarian cooperation and equality, a society which allows and promotes the creativity present in all people and especially our youth.

"Number one. An immediate end to the war in Vietnam and a restructuring of our foreign policy which totally eliminates aspects of military, economic and cultural imperialism; the withdrawal of all foreign based troops and the abolition of military draft.

"Two. An immediate freedom for Huey Newton of the Black Panthers and all other black people; adoption of the community control concept in our ghetto areas; an end to the cultural and economic domination of minority groups.

"Three. The legalization of marijuana and all other psychedelic drugs; the freeing of all prisoners currently imprisoned on narcotics charges.

"Number four. A prison system based on the concept of rehabilitation rather than punishment.

"Five. A judicial system which works towards the abolition of all laws related to crimes without victims; that is, retention only of laws relating to crimes in which there is an unwilling injured party: i.e. murder, rape, or assault.

"Six. The total disarmament of all the people beginning with the police. This includes not only guns but such brutal vices as tear gas, Mace, electric prods, blackjacks, billy clubs, and the like.

"Seven. The abolition of money, the abolition of pay housing, pay media, pay transportation, pay food, pay education, pay clothing, pay medical health, and pay toilets.

"Eight. A society which works towards and actively promotes the concept of full unemployment, a society in which people are free from the drudgery of work, adoption of the concept 'Let the machines do it.'

"Number ten. A program of ecological development that would provide incentives for the decentralization of crowded cities and encourage rural living.

"Eleven. A program which provides not only free birth control information and devices, but also abortions when desired.

"Twelve. A restructured educational system which provides a student power to determine his course of study, student participation in over-all policy planning; an educational system which breaks down its barriers between school and community; a system which uses the surrounding community as a classroom so that students may learn directly the problems of the people.

"Number thirteen. The open and free use of the media; a program which actively supports and promotes cable television as a method of increasing the selection of channels available to the viewer.

"Fourteen. An end to all censorship. We are sick of a society that has no hesitation about showing people committing violence and refuses to show a couple fucking.

"Fifteen. We believe that people should fuck all the time, any time, wherever they wish. This is not a programmed demand but a simple recognition of the reality around us.

"Sixteen. A political system which is more streamlined and responsive to the needs of all the people regardless of age, sex, or race; perhaps a national referendum system conducted via television or a telephone voting system; perhaps a decentralization of power and authority with many varied tribal groups, groups in which people exist in a state of basic trust and are free to choose their tribe.

"Seventeen. A program that encourages and promotes the arts. However, we feel that if the free society we envision were to be sought for and achieved, all of us would actualize the creativity within us; in a very real sense we would have a society in which every man would be an artist.'

And eighteen was left blank for anybody to fill in what they wanted.

"It was for these reasons that we had come to Chicago, it was for these reasons that many of us may fight and die here. We recognize this as the vision of the founders of this nation. We recognize that we are America; we recognize that we are free men. The present-day politicians and their armies of automatons have selfishly robbed us of our birthright. The evilness they stand for will go unchallenged no longer. Political pigs, your days are numbered. We are the second American Revolution. We shall win.

"YIPPIE."

MR. WEINGLASS: When you used the words "fight and die here," in what context were you using those words?

THE WITNESS: It is a metaphor. That means that we felt strongly about our right to assemble in the park and that people should be willing to take risks for it. It doesn't spell it out because people were capable of fighting in their own way and making their own decisions and we never would tell anyone specifically that they should fight, fistfight.

MR. WEINGLASS: Did you during the week of the Convention and the period of time immediately before the Convention tell any person singly or in groups that they should fight in the park?

MR. SCHULTZ: Objection.

THE COURT: I sustain the objection.

MR. WEINGLASS: Directing your attention to the morning of August 19, 1968, did you attend a meeting on that day?

THE WITNESS: Yes. I went to the office of the Mobilization Committee.

MR. WEINGLASS: Was there a discussion?

THE WITNESS: I never stayed long at these meetings. I just went and made an announcement and maybe stayed ten or fifteen minutes. . . .

MR. WEINGLASS: Was there a course given in snake dancing on that day also?

THE WITNESS: Yes. Yes. People would have a pole and there would be about six people, and then about six people behind them, holding them around the waist, four or five lines of these people with men, women, and kids maybe eight years old in on this whole thing, and people would bounce from one foot to the other and yell "Wash oi, Wash oi," which is kind of Japanese for "Yippie," I guess.

And they would just march up and down the park like this, mostly laughing and giggling, because the newsmen were taking this quite seriously, and then at a certain point everybody would turn in and sort of just collapse and fall on the ground and laugh. I believe we lost about four or five Yippies during that great training.

The exciting part was when the police arrested two army intelligence officers in the trees.

MR. WEINGLASS: During the course of that day when you were in the park, did you notice that the police were hanging any signs in the park?

THE WITNESS: Late in the day, maybe four or five, I became aware that there were police nailing signs on the trees that said "11:00 p.m. curfew," maybe a few other words, but that was the gist of the signs.

MR. WEINGLASS: From Friday, August 23, on to the end of Convention week, did you ever discuss with any people the question of staying in the park after the curfew hours?

THE WITNESS: At a meeting on August 24, that subject came up, and there was lengthy discussion.

MR. WEINGLASS: Now, did you hear Jerry Rubin speak at that meeting?

THE WITNESS: Jerry said that the park wasn't worth fighting for; that we should leave at the eleven p.m. curfew. He said that we should put out a statement to that effect.

MR. WEINGLASS: And did you speak at that meeting?

THE WITNESS: I reported on a meeting that morning with Chief Lynskey. I had asked the Chicago cops who were tailing me to take me to Chief Lynskey who was in charge of the area of Lincoln Park. I went up to the chief and said, "Well, are you going to let us have the Festival?"

He said "No festival under any circumstances. If anybody breaks one city ordinance in that park, we clear the whole park."

He said, "You do any one thing wrong and I will arrest you on sight."

He said, "Why don't you try to kick me in the shins right now?"

And I said NBC wasn't there.

And he said, "Well, at least the kid's honest," and stuff like that.

Then I gave a speech to the police that were all assembled and I said, "Have a good time." I said, "The National Guard's coming in, they're probably going to whip you guys up, and I hope your walkie-talkies work better than ours," and stuff like that. And I just walked out.

Then we discussed what we were going to do. I said it was my feeling that Chicago was in a total state of anarchy as far as the police mentality worked. I said that we were going to have to fight for every single thing, we were going to have to fight for the electricity, we were going to have to fight to have the stage come in, we were going to have to fight for every rock musician to play, that the whole week was going to be like that.

I said that we should proceed with the festival as planned, we should try to do everything that we had come to Chicago to do, even though the police and the city officials were standing in our way.

MR. WEINGLASS: During the course of this Saturday and prior to this meeting, did you have occasion to meet Irv Bock [the police informant] in the park?

THE WITNESS: Oh, I met Irv Bock Saturday afternoon during some of the marshal training. Marshal training is a difficult phrase to use for Yippies. We always have a reluctance to marshals because they are telling people what to do and we were more anarchistic than that, more leaderless.

I sort of bumped into Irv Bock. I showed him a — it wasn't a gas mask but it was a thing with two plastic eyes and a little piece of leather that I got, I purchased in an army-navy store for about nineteen cents, and I said that these would be good protection against Mace.

He started running down to me all this complicated military jargon and I looked at him and said, "Irv, you're a cop, ain't you?"

He sort of smiled and said, "No, I'm not."

"Come on," I said, "We don't grow peaceniks that big. We are all quarterbacks. You've got to be a cop."

I said, "Show me your wallet."

So he said, "No, no. Don't you trust me?"

So I said, "Irv," I said, "last night there was a guy running around my house with a pistol trying to kill me," that I had twenty threats that week, and at that point I didn't trust Jerry Rubin. . . .

MR. WEINGLASS: Directing your attention to approximately two o'clock in the morning, which would now be Monday morning, do you recall what you were doing?

THE WITNESS: I made a telephone call to David Stahl, Deputy Mayor of Chicago at his home. I had his home number.

I said, "Hi, Dave. How's it going? Your police got to be the dumbest and the most brutal in the country," I said.

"The decision to drive people out of the park in order to protect the City was about the dumbest military tactic since the Trojans let the Trojan horse inside the gate and there was nothing to be compared with that stupidity."

I again pleaded with him to let people stay in the park the following night. "There will be more people coming Monday, Tuesday, and subsequently Wednesday night," I said, "and they should be allowed to sleep." I said that he ought to intercede with the Police Department. I said to him that the City officials, in particular his boss, Daley, were totally out of their minds.

I said, "I read in the paper the day before that they had 2,000 troops surrounding the reservoirs in order to protect against the Yippie plot to dump LSD in the drinking water. There isn't a kid in the country," I said, "never mind a Yippie, who thinks that such a thing could be done."

I told him to check with all the scientists at the University of Chicago—he owned them all.

He said that he knew it couldn't be done, but they weren't taking any chances anyway . . . .

MR. WEINGLASS: Can you tell the Court and jury where you were in Lincoln Park at approximately 11:30 Monday night?

THE WITNESS: I was walking through the barricade, my wife Anita and I.

MR. WEINGLASS: Did you see Allen Ginsberg at the barricade?

THE WITNESS: Yes. He was kneeling.

There was a crowd of people around. He was playing that instrument that he plays and people were chanting.

There was a police car that would come by and I believe it was making announcements and people would yell at the police car, you know, "Beat it. Get out. The parks belong to the people. Oink Oink. Pig Pig. Pigs are coming. Peace Now."

People were waving flags. People were running around being scared and people were running around sort of joyous. I mean, it was strange, different emotions. It was very dark in that place.

MR. SCHULTZ: The witness is not answering the question any more. He is giving another essay. I object.

MR. WEINGLASS: When the police finally came to the barricade, from what direction did they come?

THE WITNESS: They came in through the zoo.

They proceeded to climb and immediately started to club people.

They were throwing parts of the barricade, trashcans, at people.

MR. WEINGLASS: Now, at the time the police came to the barricade what did you do?

THE WITNESS: Well, I was coughing and spitting because there was tear gas totally flooding the air, cannisters were exploding all around me — I moved with the people out this way, out of the park trying to duck, picking up people that were being clubbed, getting off the ground myself a few times.

The police were just coming through in this wedge, solid wedge, clubbing people right and left, and I tried to get out of the park.

MR. WEINGLASS: Directing your attention to approximately six o'clock the following morning, do you recall where you were?

THE WITNESS: I got in the car of the police that were following me and asked them to take me to the beach — the beach part of Lincoln Park.

MR. WEINGLASS: What was occurring when you got there?

THE WITNESS: Allen Ginsberg and about — oh 150-200 people were kneeling, most of the people in lotus position which is a position with their legs crossed like this — chanting and praying and meditating.

There were five or six police cars on the boardwalk right in back, and there were police surrounding the group. Dawn was breaking. It was very cold, very chilly. People had a number of blankets wrapped around them, sitting in a circle. I went and sat next to Allen and chanted and prayed for about an hour. Then I talked to the group. People would give talks about their feelings of what was going on in Chicago. I said, "I am very sad about what has happened in Chicago.

"What is going on here is very beautiful, but it won't be in the evening news that night.

"The American mass media is a glutton for violence, and it would be only shots of what was happening in the streets of Chicago."

I said, "America can't be changed by people sitting and praying, and this is an unfortunate reality that we have to face."

I said that we were a community that had to learn how to survive, that we had seen what had happened the last few nights in Lincoln Park. We had seen the destruction of the Festival.

I said, "I will never again tell people to sit quietly and pray for change."...

MR. WEINGLASS: Now, directing your attention to approximately 6:00 A.M. the following morning, Wednesday, August 28, do you recall what you were doing?

THE WITNESS: I went to eat. I went with Paul Krassner, Beverly Baskinger, and Anita and four police officers— Paul also had two Chicago police officers following him, as well as the two that were following me. We walked and the four of them would drive along behind us.

MR. WEINGLASS: Could you describe for the jury and the Court what you were wearing at that time?

THE WITNESS: Well, I had cowboy boots, and brown pants and a shirt, and I had a grey felt ranger cowboy type hat down over my eyes, like this.

MR.WEINGLASS: What, if anything occurred while you were sitting there having breakfast?

THE WITNESS: Well, two policemen came in and said, "We have orders to arrest you. You have something under your hat."

So I asked them if they had a search warrant and I said 'Did you check it out with Commander Braasch? Me and him got an agreement"—and they went to check it out with him, while we were eating breakfast.

MR. WEINGLASS: After a period of time, did they come back?

THE WITNESS: They came back with more police officers— there were about four or five patrol cars surrounding the restaurant. The Red Squad cops who had been following us came in the restaurant, four or five police, and they said, "We checked. Now will you take off your hat?" They were stern, more serious about it.

MR. WEINGLASS: What did you do?

THE WITNESS: Well, I lifted up the hat and I went "Bang! Bang!"

They grabbed me by the jacket and pulled me across the bacon and eggs and Anita over the table, threw me on the floor and out the door and threw me against the car, and they handcuffed me.

I was just eating the bacon and going "Oink Oink!"

MR. WEINGLASS: Did they tell you why you were being arrested?

THE WITNESS: They said they arrested me because I had the word "Fuck" on my forehead. I had put it on with this magic marker before we left the house. They called it an "obscenary."

I put it on for a couple of reasons. One was that I was tired of seeing my picture in the paper and having newsmen come around, and I know if you got that word on your forehead they ain't going to print your picture in the paper. Secondly, it sort of summed up my attitude about the whole thing—what was going on in Chicago.

I like that four letter word—I thought it was kind of holy, actually.

MR. WEINGLASS: Abbie Hoffman, prior to coming to Chicago, from April 1968 on to the week of the Convention, did you enter into an agreement with David Dellinger, John Froines, Tom Hayden, Jerry Rubin, Lee Weiner or Rennie Davis, to come to the city of Chicago for the purpose of encouraging and promoting violence during the Convention week?

THE WITNESS: An agreement?

MR. WEINGLASS: Yes.

THE WITNESS: We couldn't agree on lunch.

MR. WEINGLASS: I have no further questions.

THE COURT: Cross-examine.

MR. SCHULTZ: Thank you, your Honor. . . .

MR. SCHULTZ: Did you see numerous instances of people attacking the Guardsmen at the Pentagon, Mr. Hoffman?

THE WITNESS. I do not believe that I saw any instances of people attacking National Guardsmen. In fact, the attitude was one of comradeship. They would talk to the National Guardsmen continuously and tell them they were not the people that they had come to confront, that they were their brothers and you don't get people to oppose their ways by attacking them.

MR. SCHULTZ: Mr. Hoffman, the Guards and the troops were trying to keep the people from entering into the Pentagon for two days, isn't that right?

THE WITNESS: I assume that they were there to guard the Pentagon from rising in the air possibly. I mean, who knows what they are there for? Were you there? You probably watched it on television and got a different impression of what was happening. That is one aspect of myth-making—you can envisualize hoardes and hoardes of people when in reality that was not what happened.

MR SCHULTZ: Did you see some people urinate on the Pentagon?

THE WITNESS: On the Pentagon itself?

MR. SCHULTZ: Or at the Pentagon?

THE WITNESS: There were over 100,000 people. People have that biological habit, you know.

MR. SCHULTZ: Did you symbolically urinate on the Pentagon, Mr. Hoffman?

THE WITNESS: I symbolically urinate on the Pentagon?

MR. SCHULTZ: Yes.

THE WITNESS: I didn't get that close. Pee on the walls of the Pentagon?

You are getting to be out of sight, actually. You think there is a law against it?

MR. SCHULTZ: Are you done, Mr. Hoffman?

THE WITNESS: I am done when you are.

MR. SCHULTZ: Did you ever state that a sense of integration possesses you and comes from pissing on the Pentagon?

THE WITNESS: I. said from combining political attitudes with biological necessity, there is a sense of integration, yes.

MR. SCHULTZ: You had a good time at the Pentagon, didn't you. Mr. Hoffman?

THE WITNESS: Yes I did. I'm having a good time now too. I feel that biological necessity now. Could I be excused for a slight recess?

THE COURT: Ladies and gentlemen of the jury, we will take a brief recess.

*(brief recess)*

MR. SCHULTZ: On the seventh of August, you told David Stahl that at your liberated area you —

THE WITNESS: What meeting was this, August 7?

MR. SCHULTZ: That's when you just flew in from New York.

THE WITNESS: Crossing state lines —

MR. SCHULTZ: At this meeting on the evening of August 7, you told Mr. Stahl that you were going to have nude-ins in your liberated zone, didn't you?

THE WITNESS: A nude-in? I don't believe I would use that phrase, no. I don't think it's very poetic, frankly. I might have told him that ten thousand people were going to walk naked on the waters of Lake Michigan, something like that.

MR. SCHULTZ: You told him, did you not, Mr. Hoffman, that in your liberated zone, you would have —

THE WITNESS: I'm not even sure what it is, a nude-in.

MR. SCHULTZ: — public fornication.

THE WITNESS: If it means ten thousand people, naked people, walking on Lake Michigan, yes.

MR.KUNSTLER: I object to this because Mr. Schultz is acting like a dirty old man.

MR. SCHULTZ: We are not going into dirty old men. If they are going to have nude-ins and public fornication, the City officials react to that, and I am establishing through this witness that that's what he did.

THE COURT: Do you object?

MR. KUNSTLER: I am just remarking, your Honor, that a young man can be a dirty old man.

THE WITNESS: I don't mind talking about it.

THE COURT: I could make an observation. I have seen some exhibits here that are not exactly exemplary documents.

MR. KUNSTLER: But they are, your Honor, only from your point of view—making a dirty word of something that can be beautiful and lovely, and—

MR. SCHULTZ: We are not litigating here, your Honor, whether sexual intercourse is beautiful or not. We are litigating whether or not the City could permit tens of thousands of people to come in and do in their parks what this man said they were going to do.

In getting people to Chicago you created your Yippie myth, isn't that right? And part of your myth was "We'll burn Chicago to the ground," isn't that right?

THE WITNESS: It was part of the myth that there were trainloads of dynamite headed for Chicago, it was part of the myth that they were going to form white vigilante groups and round up demonstrators. All these things were part of the myth. A myth is a process of telling stories, most of which ain't true.

MR. SCHULTZ: Mr. Hoffman—

Your Honor, Mr. Davis is having a very fine time here whispering at me. He has been doing it for the last twenty minutes. He moved up here when I started the examination so he could whisper in my ear. I would ask Mr. Davis, if he cannot be quiet, to move to another part of the table so that he will stop distracting me.

THE COURT: Try not to speak too loudly, Mr. Davis.

MR. DAVIS: Yes, sir.

THE COURT: Go ahead.

THE WITNESS: Go ahead, Dick.

MR. SCHULTZ: Didn't you state, Mr. Hoffman, that part of the myth that was being created to get people to come to Chicago was that "We will fuck on the beaches"?

THE WITNESS: Yes, me and Marshall McLuhan. Half of that quote was from Marshall McLuhan.

MR. SCHULTZ: "And there will be acid for all"—that was another one of your Yippie myths, isn't that right?

THE WITNESS: That was well known.

MR. SCHULTZ: By the way, was there any acid in Lincoln Park in Chicago?

THE WITNESS: In the reservoir, in the lake?

MR. SCHULTZ: No, among the people.

THE WITNESS: Well, there might have been, I don't know. It is colorless, odorless, tasteless. One can never tell. . . .

MR. SCHULTZ: The fact is, Mr. Hoffman, that what you were trying to do was to create a situation where the State and the United States Government would have to bring in the Army and bring in the National Guard during the Convention in order to protect the delegates so that it would appear that the Convention had to be held under military conditions, isn't that a fact, Mr. Hoffman?

THE WITNESS: You can do that with a yo-yo in this country. It's quite easy. You can see just from this courtroom. Look at all the troops around —

MR. SCHULTZ: Your Honor, may the answer be stricken?

THE COURT: Yes, it may go out. . . .

MR. SCHULTZ: Mr. Hoffman, in the afternoon on that Thursday you participated in a march, and then you laid down in front of an armored personnel carrier at the end of that march, at 16th or 19th on Michigan, laid down on the street?

THE WITNESS: Was that what it was? I thought it was a tank. It looked like a tank.

Do you want me to show you how I did it? Laid down in front of the tank?

MR. SCHULTZ: All right, Mr. Hoffman. Did you make any gestures of any sort?

THE WITNESS: When I was laying down? See. I went like that, lying down in front of the tank.

I had seen Czechoslovakian students do it to Russian tanks.

MR. SCHULTZ: And then you saw a Chicago police officer who appeared to be in high command because of all the things he had on his shoulders come over to the group and start leading them back toward Grant Park, didn't you?

THE WITNESS: He came and then people left — and went back to the park, yes.

MR. SCHULTZ: Did you say to anybody, "Well, you see that cat?", pointing to Deputy Superintendent Rochford. "When we get to the top of the hill, if the cat doesn't talk right, we're going to hold him there, and then we can do whatever we want and the police won't bother us." Did you say that to anybody out there, Mr. Hoffman?

MR. WEINGLASS: That's the testimony of the intelligence officer, the intelligence police officer of the Chicago Police Department.

THE WITNESS: I asked the Chicago police officers to help me kidnap Deputy Superintendent Rochford? That's pretty weird.

MR. SCHULTZ: Isn't it a fact that you announced publicly a plan to kidnap the head pig —

THE WITNESS: Cheese, wasn't it?

MR. SCHULTZ: — and then snuff him —

THE WITNESS: I thought it was "cheese."

MR. SCHULTZ: — and then snuff him if other policemen touched you? Isn't that a fact, sir?

THE WITNESS: I do not believe that I used the reference of "pig" to any policemen in Chicago including some of the top cheeses. I did not use it during that week. . .

MR. SCHULTZ: You and Albert, Mr. Hoffman, were united in Chicago in your determination to smash the system by using any means at your disposal, isn't that right?

THE WITNESS: Did I write that?

MR. SCHULTZ: No, did you have that thought?

THE WITNESS: That thought? Is a thought like a dream? If I dreamed to smash the system, that's a thought. Yes, I had that thought.

THE COURT: Mr. Witness, you may not interrogate the lawyer who is examining you.

THE WITNESS: Judge, you have always told people to describe what they see or what they hear. I'm the only one that has to describe what I think.

MR. WEINGLASS: I object to any reference to what a person thought or his being tried for what he thought. He may be tried for his intent.

THE COURT: Overrule the objection.

THE WITNESS: Well, I had a lot of dreams at night. One of the dreams might have been that me and Stew were united.

MR. SCHULTZ: Mr. Hoffman, isn't it a fact that one of the reasons why you came to Chicago was simply to wreck American society?

THE WITNESS: My feeling at the time, and still is, that society is going to wreck itself. I said that on a number of occasions, that our role is to survive while the society comes tumbling down around us; our role is to survive.

We have to learn how to defend ourselves, given this type of society, because of the war in Vietnam, because of racism, because of the attack on the cultural revolution—in fact because of this trial.

MR. SCHULTZ: Mr. Hoffman, by Thursday, the twenty-ninth, the last day of the Convention, you knew you had smashed the Democrats' chances for victory, isn't that a fact?

THE WITNESS: No. My attitude was it was a type of psychic jujitsu where the people smash themselves—or the party wrecks themselves. The same way this trial is.

MR. SCHULTZ: By Thursday there was no doubt in your mind when you saw the acceptance speech that you had won, and there would be a pig in the White House in '69?

THE WITNESS: Well, that was our role in coming here, to nominate a pig. That pig did win. He didn't actually—which one did?

MR. SCHULTZ: And you went out for champagne, and you brought it back to Mobilization headquarters and toasted the revolution, you did just that, right?

THE WITNESS: We drank some champagne. It was warm, warm champagne.

MR. SCHULTZ: And toasted to your success, to your victory, isn't that right?

---

THE WITNESS: We toasted to the fact that we were still alive.

That was the miracle as far as I saw it, is still being alive by that last Thursday.

MR. SCHULTZ: That's all, your Honor.

THE WITNESSS: Right on!

THE COURT: Have you finished your cross-examination?

MR. SCHULTZ: Yes, I have.

THE WITNESS: Right on!

# Testimony Of Rennie Davis

MR. WEINGLASS: Will you please identify yourself for the record?

THE WITNESS: Rennie Davis.

MR. WEINGLASS: Do you recall the first time you came to the city of Chicago?

THE WITNESS: The first time I came to the city of Chicago was to visit the international Amphitheatre in a poultry judging contest in 1956. It was the international contest and I had just won the Eastern United States Poultry Judging Contest in 4-H and I came to Chicago to participate at the International Amphitheatre in the contest here.

MR. WEINGLASS: How old were you at that time?

THE WITNESS: I was, I guess, sixteen.

MR. WEINGLASS: Your present age?

THE WITNESS: Twenty-nine.

MR. WEINGLASS: What is your occupation?

THE WITNESS: Since 1967 my primary work and concern has been ending the war in Vietnam. Until the time of this trial I was the national coordinator for the National Mobilization to End the War in Vietnam.

MR. WEINGLASS: Now, directing your attention to the early evening of November 20, 1967, do you recall where you were on that night?

THE WITNESS: I was at the University of Chicago in an auditorium called Judd Hall. It was a meeting of a group called The Resistance. I was a speaker with Bob Ross and David Harris who is the husband of Joan Baez.

MR. WEINGLASS: Could you relate now to the Court and jury the words that you spoke, as best you can recall, on that particular night?

THE WITNESS: I began by holding up a small steel ball that was green, about the size of a tennis ball and I said, "This bomb was dropped on a city of 100,000 people, a city called Nam Ding, which is about sixty-five miles south of Hanoi."

I said, "It was dropped by an American fighter jet, an F-105," and that when this bomb exploded over Nam Ding, about 640 of these round steel balls were spewed into the sky. And I said, "When this ball strikes a building or the ground or slows up in any way, these hammers are released, an explosion occurs which sends out about 300 steel pellets."

"Now one of these balls," I explained, "was roughly three times the power of an old fashioned hand grenade and with 640 of these bombs going off, you can throw steel pellets over an area about a thousand yards long, and about 250 yards wide.

"Every living thing exposed in that 1000-yard area from this single bomb, ninety percent of every living thing in that area will die," I said, "whether it's a water buffalo or a water buffalo boy."

I said that if this bomb were to go off in this room tonight, everyone in the room here would die, but as quickly as we could remove the bodies from the room, we could have another discussion about Vietnam.

I said "This bomb would not destroy this lecture podium, it would not damage the walls, the ceiling, the floor." I said, "if it is dropped on a city, it takes life but leaves the institutions. It is the ideal weapon, you see, for the mentality who reasons that life is less precious than property."

I said that in 1967, the year that we are in, one out of every two bombs dropped on North Vietnam was this weapon. One out of every two. And in 1967 the American Government told the American public that in North Vietnam it was only bombing steel and concrete.

Then I said, "I went to Vietnam not as a representative of the government and not as a member of the military but as an American citizen who was deeply perturbed that we lived in a country where our own government was lying to American people about this war. The American government claimed to be hitting only military targets. Yet what I saw was pagodas that had been gutted, schoolhouses that had been razed, population centers that had been leveled."

Then I said that I am going to the Democratic National Convention because I want the world to know that there are thousands of young people in this country who do not want to see a rigged convention rubber stamp another four years of Lyndon Johnson's war.

MR. WEINGLASS: I show you an object marked D-325 for identification and can you identify that object?

THE WITNESS: Yes. This was the bomb that I brought back from Vietnam.

MR. WEINGLASS: If the Court please, the defense would like to offer into evidence D-325, the antipersonnel bomb identified by the witness as the object held by him on the night in question.

MR. FORAN: Your honor, the Government objects to this exhibit for the following reasons. The Vietnamese war, your honor, has nothing whatsoever to do with the charges in this indictment. The Vietnamese war, which is a major difficulty of this country and a major concern of every citizen in this country, has nothing whatever to do with whether or not people in the United States have a right to travel in interstate commerce to incite a riot.

The methods and techniques of warfare have nothing whatever to do with that charge. The methods and techniques of the seeking of the end of the Vietnam war have nothing to do with the charges of this indictment.

The very purpose of the governmental system of the United States is to handle in a purposeful way within the Constitution of the United States the disposition of such complex and difficult and tragic problems that this nation has lived with for about two hundred years. The charges in this indictment your Honor, have nothing to do with this type of testimony or this kind of concept, and for that reason your Honor, the Government objects.

THE COURT: Objection sustained.

MR. KUNSTLER: Your Honor, at this point I would like to move for a mistrial

THE COURT: I deny the motion.

MR. RUBIN: You haven't heard it yet.

THE COURT: Oh, there is no ground for a mistrial.

MR. KUNSTLER: But, your Honor —

THE COURT: I direct the marshal to have this man sit down.

MR. KUNSTLER: Every time I make a motion am I going to be thrown in my seat when I argue it?

MR. DELLINGER: Force and violence. The judge is inciting a riot by asking the marshal to have him sit down.

THE COURT: That man's name is Dellinger?

MARSHAL JONESON: Will you be quiet, Mr. Dellinger?

MR. DELLINGER: After such hypocrisy I don't particularly feel like being quiet. I said before the judge was the chief prosecutor, and he's proved the point.

THE COURT: Will you remain quiet? Will you remain quiet, sir?

MR. DELLINGER: You let Foran give a foreign policy speech, but when he tries to answer it, you interrupt him and won't let him speak.

There's no pretense of fairness in this court. All you're doing is employing a riot — employing force and violence to try to keep me quiet. Just like you gagged Bobby Seale because you couldn't afford to listen to the truth that he was saying to you. You're accusing me. I'm a pacifist.

MARSHAL JONESON: Sit down, please, and be quiet.

MR. DELLINGER: I am employing nonviolence, and you're accusing me of violence, and you have a man right here, backed up by guns, jails, and force and violence. That is the difference between us.

MARSHAL JONESON: Will you sit down?

*(applause)*

THE COURT: Will you continue, please, with the direct examination of this witness?

MR. DELLINGER: There goes the violence right there.

MR. KUNSTLER: That's the Government in operation, your Honor, as it has been throughout this trial.

THE WITNESS: Your Honor, that's my sister they are taking out of the courtroom.

THE COURT: Even your sister—

MR. RUBIN: Bill, they are taking out my wife.

*(cries of "Hey, stop it!")*

MR. KUNSTLER: Your Honor, must we always have this, the force and power of the Government?

MR. FORAN: Your Honor—

MR. RUBIN: They are dragging out my wife—will you please—

THE COURT: We must have order in the courtroom.

MR. FORAN: Your Honor, traditionally in American law, cases are tried in a courtroom by the participants in the trial, not the audience, not spectators, not by shouting and screaming. This is the American judicial system, and it's worked very well for two hundred years, and it's not going to change now for these people.

MR. DELLINGER: Yes, kept the black people in slavery for two hundred years and wiped out the Indians, and kept the poor people in problems and started the war in Vietnam which is killing off at least a hundred Americans and a thousand Vietnamese every week, and we are trying to stop it.

MARSHAL JONESON: Sit down.

MR. DELLINGER: And you call that ranting and raving and screaming because we speak the truth.

MARSHAL JONESON: Mr. Dellinger, sit down, please.

MR. FORAN: Your Honor, in the American system there is a proper way to raise such issues and to correct them.

MR. DELLINGER: That was the proper way with Fred Hampton, wasn't it?

MR. FORAN: And to correct them, your Honor, by the proper governmental system, and there is a proper way to do that.

MR. KUNSTLER: This is as to Mr. Rubin's wife. She was thrown out of the courtroom, and he is a defendant here. We would like her returned to the courtroom.

THE COURT: No. As long as the marshals are in charge of the behavior of spectators in this courtroom, they will determine who misbehaves.

MR. RUBIN: Am I entitled to a public trial?

THE COURT: No—you have a public trial.

MR. RUBIN: Does a public trial include my wife being in the courtroom? Am I entitled to a public trial?

THE COURT: I don't talk to defendants who have a lawyer.

MR. RUBIN: You didn't listen to my lawyer, so I have to speak. Am I entitled to a public trial?

THE COURT: You may continue with the direct examination of this witness. If you don't, I will just have to ask him to get off the witness stand.

MR. WEINGLASS: Your Honor, the witness has seen from his vantage point his sister forcibly taken from this room. I wonder if we could have a short recess to resolve that?

THE COURT: No recess. No, no. There will be no recess, sir. You will proceed to examine this witness.

MR. WEINGLASS: I direct your attention to February 11, 1968, do you recall where you were?

THE WITNESS: I was in Chicago at what later became the Mobilization office, 407 South Dearborn.

MR. WEINGLASS: What was occurring in the office?

THE WITNESS: I believe it was a planning meeting to talk about the conference that I had requested of the National Mobilization, a bringing together of all groups interested in Chicago.

MR. WEINGLASS: Did you talk about Chicago?

THE WITNESS: Yes. I said that the key questions before us today was what to do in Chicago, what to do at the Convention itself. Then I listed four positions that I proposed as a kind of agenda.

I said position number one would be we should go to the Democratic Convention to disrupt it.

I said there may be people in this room who do believe that the Democratic Convention, which is responsible for the war, should be physically disrupted, torn apart. I said I don't think that is the MOBE's position—but I think that it is essential that we put it on the agenda. It is an issue that has been created in the press and that we vote it up or down so that we can make ourselves clear on this issue.

So issue position number one would be disrupt the Convention.

Position number two, I said, that has been talked about, is that the peace movement should support a candidate. Maybe we should support Eugene McCarthy.

Then I said position number three, that had been talked about by some organizations, was what we called stay-home. This was a position that said that Daley is so concerned about the Convention and having demonstrators come into Chicago that he'd bring in the troops, he'd bring in the police, he'd start cracking heads. And in fact this might play right into Johnson's hands. It might show that the Democratic Party is the party of law and order.

So I said position three, that we should talk about here, is whether or not we should have a demonstration at all.

Then I said position number four is a campaign that begins in the spring, it goes into the fall, it goes into the summer, and then finally brings to Chicago literally every possible constituency of the American people.

MR. WEINGLASS: Now, after you outlined these four alternatives, did you say anything further about them then?

THE WITNESS: Well, there was a very long discussion of these four proposals, and I guess at the end of that discussion I said that it was clear that in this meeting of representatives of major national groups across the country there was not a single person who did not favor position number four.

Then Tom interrupted me, and he said he thought that was wrong.

A group of so-called leaders of organizations shouldn't just get together and decide what position to present to everyone. Tom thought that we should now talk about calling a very large conference of organizations to consider all four alternatives, and then he said that each one of these positions should be written up in a paper and presented to — to this conference.

MR. WEINGLASS: Was such a conference called?

THE WITNESS: Yes, it was. It took place at a place called Lake Villa. It was a YMCA camp, just beside a big lake.

MR. WEINGLASS: Now I show you a document which has been marked D-235 for identification, and I ask you if you can identify that document?

THE WITNESS: Yes, I can. Tom Hayden and I wrote this paper. It's called, "Movement Campaign 1968, an Election Year Offensive."

The paper was mimeographed in our office and then presented to every delegate at this Lake Villa meeting outside of Chicago. This was alternative number four that was agreed upon.

MR. WEINGLASS: I offer into evidence D-235 as Defendant's Exhibit Number D-235.

THE COURT: Show it to counsel.

MR. FORAN: Your Honor, this document was offered once before. This document is some twenty-one pages in length. It contains in it a number of broad summary statements that are not supported by factual data.

Each statement in itself has elements in it that are both irrelevant summary statements of a gross character totally unprovable by evidence, and self-serving in nature, and the law, your Honor, is clear that a self-serving declaration of an act or a party is inadmissible in evidence in his favor.

MR. WEINGLASS: If the Court please, the first time this document was offered, it was through the testimony of the witness Meacham. At that time the Government objected on the ground that the authors of the document were the only persons who could qualify the document for admission. The author is now on the stand, and of course now we are met with the objection that it is self-serving.

If you deny this document then you are proceeding on the assumption, your Honor, that the defendants are guilty and they are contriving documents. That has to be the beginning premise of your thinking if you feel this document is self-serving. If they are innocent, which is what the presumption is supposed to be—then I don't know why the Court would consider that this document would be possibly contrived.

THE COURT: You have here as a witness a very articulate, well-educated, seemingly intelligent witness; why can't he be questioned about his participation in the composition of that document?

MR. WEINGLASS: The defendants are entitled to the benefit of all of the legal evidence they have indicating their innocence, writings as well as spoken words. If this document contained plans to bomb the Amphitheatre or to create a disturbance or riot in the city streets, we clearly would have had this document in evidence in the Government's case, but it contains the contrary and that is why it is being offered. I think they are entitled to the benefit of anything that indicates their innocence as well as their guilt.

THE COURT: I shall not take it in. I sustain the objection of the Government.

MR. WEINGLASS: Your Honor has read the document?

THE COURT: I have looked it over.

THE WITNESS: You never read it. I was watching you. You read two pages.

THE COURT: Mr. Marshal, will you instruct that witness on the witness stand that he is not to address me.

You may continue sir, with your direct examination.

MR. WEINGLASS: Without referring to the document, what did you say about Chicago, if anything?

MR. FORAN: Your Honor, the form of the question is bad.

THE COURT: I sustain the objection.

MR. WEINGLASS: Did you have occasion to speak at the conference?

THE WITNESS: Yes, I spoke at a workshop Saturday evening. Tom and I were both present because we were presenting our paper.

MR. WEINGLASS: Could you relate to the Court and to the jury what you said at the workshop respecting Chicago?

THE WITNESS: Tom spoke about the paper and what was in it and then someone asked Tom why there was an entire page devoted to the issue about disruption and I answered that question.

MR. WEINGLASS: Do you recall your answer?

THE WITNESS: I said that the reason that this document devotes so much attention to the question of violence and disruption at the Convention is because we think that this is not a demonstration where simply the peace movement comes to Chicago. This is, rather, a demonstration where the peace movement is the instrument to bring literally hundreds of thousands of people to Chicago, and I said that is why it is necessary to make crystal clear our position on disruption.

And I said that is why we feel that we have bent over backwards in this document to make our position on violence and disruption very clear, and we think that we should argue with every organization in the country who is for peace that that must be the strategy in Chicago.

MR. WEINGLASS: Now, directing your attention to the twentieth of July, 1968, do you recall where you were?

THE WITNESS: I was in Cleveland, Ohio, at a meeting in a church in Cleveland.

MR. WEINGLASS: Were any of the other defendants seated here at the table present?

THE WITNESS: Both Dave and Tom were present.

MR. WEINGLASS: Did you speak at that meeting?

THE WITNESS: Yes, I did. I said that I thought what was happening in Chicago was that our original plan to bring a half million American citizens to Chicago was so upsetting to the Mayor of Chicago, who was hosting a Convention of his own party, that there was a real danger that the Mayor had made a decision somewhere along the line to try to scare people away, to try to reduce the numbers of people expected, by stalling on permits and through suggesting that anybody who came to Chicago was going to be clubbed or beaten or Maced.

I said, "On the other hand, I don't want to discourage people into thinking that we are not going to get permits. There are several things in the works that give me a considerable amount of optimism".....

MR. WEINGLASS: Directing your attention to the morning of August 2, 1968, do you recall where you were?

THE WITNESS: I was at the Palmer House, at the coffee shop in the basement. I was meeting with David Stahl, the deputy mayor of the City of Chicago, and with me was Mark Simons.

MR. WEINGLASS: Do you recall, did a conversation occur between yourself and David Stahl?

THE WITNESS: Yes, it did. I said that I felt that given the reports that we had seen in the past, that there was some question about our purposes and intentions in coming to Chicago. I said I did not understand any other explanation for the military sort of saber rattling that was going on at that time, the constant talks in the past about disruption of the Convention.

I indicated that the character of the demonstration that was planned by our coalition was not like the Pentagon, where civil disobedience was called for, but was more like the character of the April 15 demonstration in New York, where we hoped to be effective in our protest by numbers and not by militant tactics.

I said that I thought the problem areas that we had to work out were, first of all, the matter of a march and an assembly to the Amphitheatre, and that when we had applied for a permit for the use of Halsted, that that was negotiable and that we have at this point not even applied for how to get to Halsted because we wanted to make this an open meeting between you and me.

I then said that the second area of concern for us was the whole matter of parks, that we thought that integral to our program was having park space set aside by City officials so that people could meet and sleep throughout the week of the Convention.

Then Mr. Stahl indicated to me that he thought it might be difficult for the city to grant a permit for the use of a park; that there was a curfew at 11:00 p.m., and that this would be a violation of a city ordinance to give a permit for park space beyond 11:00 p.m.

Mr. Stahl was not sure what the feeling of the City would be with respect to an assembly at the Amphitheatre. I said I thought it was very dangerous for us to even consider an area not adjacent to the Amphitheatre, because people on their own would then go down to the area, they would not have marshals, they would not have organization, and the possibility of disruption and violence would be very great.

Then Mr. Stahl said that he agreed, that it probably would create less problems if people did not march as pedestrians but went in an orderly group.

I then asked him, "Well, how do we begin to talk about these matters?"

And he said, that the mayor's office was not responsible for granting of permits, that these matters were the responsibility of the Park District, the Streets and Sanitation Department and the Police Department and the other agencies directly involved, and then I said, "Mr. Stahl, you're not dealing with an out-of-towner. I live in Chicago, and you can say this to the press, but I really wish you wouldn't say it to me." I said, "Everyone knows in this town who makes decisions like this. You can't tell me that the Streets and Sanitation Department head that's appointed by Mayor Daley is going to make a decision independent of the Mayor," and he sort of smiled at that point and didn't say anything.

Mr. Stahl was very cordial at the end and said, "Thank you very much for what you've said, and I'll relate this back to the appropriate bodies."

MR. WEINGLASS: At approximately six o'clock that night, still on August 21, 1968, do you recall where you were?

THE WITNESS: I was on my way to the Mobilization executive committee meeting, an apartment in Hyde Park.

MR. WEINGLASS: As you were outside, about to enter the apartment, did you have occasion to meet with anyone?

THE WITNESS: Yes. I met with Irv Bock.

MR. WEINGLASS: Now, without going into your conversation with Mr. Bock just now, do you recall what Mr. Bock had in his hand, if anything?

THE WITNESS: He went to his car and he came back and he had—it is hard to describe. It was a very large balloon, and attached to the balloon was a small tube, and stuck in the tube was a cloth fiber, and he took the glass tube and put it into some water, and the air from the balloon would pass through the glass tube in what appeared to be a regular way, so that one bubble would come up and then another and then another and then another, and he explained how this worked.

MR. WEINGLASS: What did he say to you?

THE WITNESS: Well, he said that with this device it's possible to fill the balloon with helium gas and to launch the balloon in the air and allow the helium gas to come out of the balloon in a way that can be computed mathematically so that you know when all of the air will be out of the balloon, and by computing the velocity it's possible to send the balloon up in the air and figure out exactly where it will fall. I said, "Why in the world would anyone be interested in that?"

And he said, "Well, you can attach anything that you want to this balloon, send it up into the air, and then we can drop it on the International Amphitheatre."

And I said, "Well, what would you want to attach to the balloon?" And he said, "Anything you want."

I thanked Irv for his suggestion and went inside.

MR. WEINGLASS: Now, on August 4, do you recall where you were?

THE WITNESS: Yes. I was at a Mobilization steering committee meeting just outside of Chicago. It was in Highland Park at a sort of old fancy hotel that disgusted me. I mean, it was fancy, so I didn't like it.

MR. WEINGLASS: Now, at noon of that day, do you recall where you were?

THE WITNESS: There was a lunch break around noon or 12:30, and the meeting emptied out down towards the lake. I was on a sandy beach on the edge of Lake Michigan, eating my lunch.

MR. WEINGLASS: Were you alone?

THE WITNESS: No, there were a number of people. Irv Bock was present. Well, Tom Hayden, really, and I were together and we talked and ate lunch together.

MR. WEINGLASS: And did you have a conversation with Tom Hayden on the beach?

THE WITNESS: Yes. I told Tom that I had received a letter from Don Duncan who was a close friend of ours and Don had sent us sort of a list of the various kinds of gases that were being used by the Army in South Vietnam. He described in some detail a gas called CS, which he said caused extreme congestion of the chest, a burning sensation in the face, the eyes filled with tears. Actual burns could occur on the face from this, and in heavy dosage, it could cause death.

Don said that he had information that these kinds of new chemicals being used on the people of Vietnam were now going to be used on the peace movement, and he was especially concerned that this might be the case in Chicago.

MR. WEINGLASS: When you and Tom Hayden had that conversation, did you notice the whereabouts of Irv Bock?

THE WITNESS: He was there. I mean, he was close by.

MR. WEINGLASS: Directing your attention to August 13, in the evening at approximately six o'clock, did you have occasion to speak with anyone?

THE WITNESS: I spoke with my attorney, Irving Birnbaum, by phone.

MR. WEINGLASS: Do you recall that conversation you had with him on the phone?

THE WITNESS: Yes. I said, "Irv, things are going very badly with permits. This morning the Park District met. I absolutely cannot understand it. Mr. Barry promised us it was going to be on the agenda and it was not even brought up in the meeting."

I said in addition to that, "Yesterday we had a meeting with David Stahl and Richard Elrod where all of the agency heads were supposed to attend, and none of them did." I said that "I feel, very frankly, that the Mayor is now using the permit issue as a kind of political device to scare people away." And I said, "Very frankly, he's being extremely effective."

I then asked Irv whether or not he thought it made sense to file some kind of lawsuit against the City and take this whole question of permits into the courts.

Irv then said that he thought that would be a practical proposal, that we should draw up a lawsuit against the City, that the City is using its administrative control over permits to deny fundamental First Amendment and Constitutional rights. I then said to Irv that Mr. Elrod has been quite emphatic with me about the matter of sleeping in the parks beyond 11:00 p.m. "Do we have any legal basis," I said, "for staying in the parks beyond 11:00?"

Irv Birnbaum said that he thought that very definitely that should be included in the lawsuit because he said that parks were made available for the Boy Scouts and for National Guard troops beyond 11:00 p.m., and that under the Civil Rights Act of equal protection under the law, the same kind of facilities should be made available to American citizens, and he indicated that this should be put in the lawsuit.

MR. WEINGLASS: The following Sunday, which was August 18, do you recall where you were in the morning of that day?

THE WITNESS: Yes. In the morning I was at a union hall on Nobel Street. We were having a meeting of the steering committee of the Mobilization.

MR. WEINGLASS: Were there any other defendants present?

THE WITNESS: Yes. John Froines was present.

MR. WEINGLASS: Do you recall what John Froines said at that particular meeting?

THE WITNESS: I recall that John reported on our work with marshals. He said that we were well under way with training sessions in Lincoln Park.

He then went on to talk about some of the problems that we were having, concerns about police violence, the fact that we were going to have to be very mobile through this week if the police came in to break up demonstrations.

I think at one point he said, "We may have to be as mobile as a guerrilla, moving from place to place in order to avoid arrest and avoid police confrontation."

MR. WEINGLASS: Mr. Davis, directing your attention to Wednesday, August 21, at about 10:30 in the morning, do you recall where you were?

THE WITNESS: I was in this building, in Judge Lynch's chambers.

MR. WEINGLASS: Now, who went with you into the Judge's chambers?

THE WITNESS: An attorney, who was assisting the National Mobilization Committee, Stanley Bass. I believe that Richard Elrod was present, Ray Simon, the Corporation Counsel, was present. Judge Lynch, of course, and others.

MR. WEINGLASS: Could you relate to the Court and jury specific conversations in connection with that lawsuit?

THE WITNESS: Well, Mr. Simon proposed to the Mobilization a number of assembly areas for our consideration. He said he made these proposals rather than the one that we suggested because he thought it unreasonable of the Mobilization to insist on a State Street march, that this would disrupt traffic too much.

I then told Mr. Simon that I thought these proposals were quite generous, and I was certain that on this matter we could reach an accommodation.

I said, "The problem with your proposal. Mr. Simon, is that it does not address itself to the fundamental issue for us, which is an assembly in the area of the Amphitheatre at the time of the Democratic nomination."

I went on to say that I would make two concrete proposals at this time. I said that it would be satisfactory to our coalition to consider the area on Halsted Street from 39th on the north to 47th on the south.

I said if that was not acceptable to the City, that there's a large area just west of the parking lot, that would be suitable for our purposes, and I thought would not interfere with the delegates.

Mr. Simons then said that the area on Halsted from 39th on the north to 45th on the south was out of the question for consideration, that it was a security area, he said, and that it was not possible for the City to grant this area to the Mobilization.

He then said that the second area that I had proposed similarly was out of the question because I think he said it was controlled by the Democratic National Convention and the City had no authority to grant that space to the Mobilization.

Then I said, "Assuming both of these areas are just not available, could you, Mr. Simon, suggest an area that would be within eyeshot of the Amphitheatre for an assembly on the evening of the nomination?"

Mr. Simon then said he didn't see why we needed to have an assembly area within eyeshot or close to the Amphitheatre. He said that the City was willing to make other proposals for such an assembly, they would offer us Grant Park, they would offer us Lincoln Park, they would offer us Garfield Park on the west side of Chicago.

MR. WEINGLASS: Now, can you remember where you were in the afternoon of Friday, the twenty-third of August?

THE WITNESS: I think I was in the Mobilization office at that time.

MR. WEINGLASS: Did you receive a phone call at approximately that time in the office?

THE WITNESS: Yes, I did. It was my attorney, Mr. Birnbaum. He said to me that the had just received the opinion of Judge Lynch denying us a permit for an assembly and denying us the right to use parks beyond 11:00 p.m. I then said, "We should appeal this matter immediately. We are in absolute crisis."

Then Mr. Birnbaum said that, in his professional opinion, no appeal would produce a permit in time for our activities during the week of the Convention, but that he was willing to draw up the papers for appeal for the purpose of preserving the record.

MR. WEINGLASS: I show you D-339 for identification, which is a photograph. Can you identify the persons in that photograph?

THE WITNESS: Myself, Tom Hayden and one of the police tails who followed me through much of the convention week, Ralph Bell.

MR. WEINGLASS: Do you recall when you first saw Mr. Bell, the police tail?

THE WITNESS: Well, on Friday after the phone call from Irv Birnbaum, I then walked out of the building, just to take a long walk alone and to think about what I personally was going to do during this week, and when I came back into the building, there were two men in sort of casual clothes who approached me at the elevator door and flashed badges, said they were policemen, and they were coming up to the office. I went back into the office and they waited outside, and I got Tom, and Tom and I then went back out to talk with them.

MR. WEINGLASS: Could you relate to the Court and jury the conversation that you and Tom Hayden had?

THE WITNESS: Well, one of the gentlemen just flashed his badge for the second time and said, "My name's Officer Bell.

This here's Riggio. We're gonna be around you a lot, Davis, so we'll just be around you and going wherever you go from now until the Convention's over," and I said, "Well, what's the purpose of this?"

And Bell said, "Well, the purpose is to give you protection," and I said, "Well, thank you very much, but I'd just as soon not have your protection."

And then Bell said, "Well, just pretend like you're President and got protection everywhere you go, day and night," and I said, "Well, what if I would request not to have this protection."

And then he said, "Motherfucker, you got the protection, and you try to shake me and you're in big trouble. Now, you cooperate, and we'll get along real fine, hear?"

And I said, "Yes, sir," and walked back into the office.

MR. WEINGLASS: I draw your attention to Monday, August 26, at approximately 2:30 in the afternoon of that day. Do you recall where you were?

THE WITNESS: Well, that afternoon, Monday, I was in Lincoln Park.

MR. WEINGLASS: When Tom Hayden was arrested, were you at the scene of the arrest?

THE WITNESS: No, sir, I was not. I was in the park at the time, yes.

MR. WEINGLASS: Now, when did you first become aware of the fact that he had been arrested?

THE WITNESS: It was around 2:30. A number of people came to me and said that Tom Hayden and Wolfe Lowenthal had been arrested and I could see the people sort of were spontaneously coming together. Many people were talking about marching on to the police station in response to this arrest.

MR. WEINGLASS: And then after receiving that information, what did you do?

THE WITNESS: Well, I talked to a number of marshals about the urgency of getting on with this march and trying to see that it has direction and that our marshals are involved in this march. I was just sort of concerned that people not run out into the streets and down to the police station, so I got on the bullhorn and started to urge people to gather behind the sound for the march to the police station.

MR. WEINGLASS: Approximately how many people joined the march?

THE WITNESS: Well, my recollection is hazy—over a thousand people, I think, joined the march. I was marching about four or five rows from the front with the sound.

MR. WEINGLASS: Were any defendants in your company at that time?

THE WITNESS: Yes. John Froines was with me, really throughout the march that day.

MR. WEINGLASS: And was this march proceeding on the sidewalk, or was it in the roadway?

THE WITNESS: No, it was on the sidewalk, all the way across the sidewalk until a police officer requested that I urge people to stay on one half of the sidewalk.

MR. WEINGLASS: Now, as you were proceeding south on State Street, were you in the company of any officials of the city of Chicago?

THE WITNESS: Yes. I was in the company of two members of the Corporation Counsel, one of whom was Richard Elrod.

MR. WEINGLASS: As you approached the police station, did you have occasion to speak again to Mr. Elrod?

THE WITNESS: Yes. About a block away from the police station, I spoke with Mr. Elrod. I said, "Mr. Elrod, the police station is completely encircled with uniformed police officers. I'm attempting to move the people out of that area and move past the police station, but you've created a situation where we have to move demonstrators down a solid wall of policemen.

"All that has to happen is for one demonstrator to strike a policeman or for one policeman to be too anxious walking past that line, and we've got a full-scale riot on our hands. I'm just not moving this line until those policemen are taken back into that building." And at that point Mr. Elrod said well, he'd see what he could do.

MR. WEINGLASS: Did you observe what Mr. Elrod did after that conversation?

THE WITNESS: I didn't see what he did, but minutes later the policemen in formation marched back into the police headquarters at 11th and State.

MR. WEINGLASS: After the police went back into the police headquarters building what did you do?

THE WITNESS: I urged people to march past the police station staying on the sidewalk, staying together, and I think we began to chant "Free Hayden." We continued then east on 11th Street toward Michigan Avenue, and north on the sidewalk on Michigan.

MR. WEINGLASS: As you were proceeding north, what, if anything, did you observe?

THE WITNESS: To the best of my recollection the march had stopped while we were waiting for the other participants to catch up and it was at that moment that some of the people in the demonstration just sort of broke out of the line of march and ran up a hill, the top of which had the statue of General Jonathan Logan.

MR. WEINGLASS: At that time that the demonstrators broke from the line of march and ran up the hill, were you speaking on the microphone?

THE WITNESS: Not at the time that they broke, no. I had stopped and was waiting for the rest of the people to catch up.

MR. WEINGLASS: Were these people carrying anything in their hands?

THE WITNESS: Yes. They were carrying flags of all kinds, Viet Cong flags, red flags.

MR. WEINGLASS: After you saw them run up the hill to the statue, what, if anything, did you do?

THE WITNESS: A police formation developed at the base of the hill and began to sweep upward toward the statue and at that point I yelled very loudly that people should leave the statue and go to the Conrad Hilton. I said a number of things very rapidly like, "We have liberated the statue, now we should go to the Conrad Hilton. The Conrad Hilton is the headquarters of the people who are responsible for the arrest. Let's leave the statue, let's liberate the Hilton," basically urging people to get away from the statue.

MR. FORAN: I object to the characterization of the words, your Honor.

THE COURT: The use of the word "urging"?

MR. FORAN: "Basically," from the word "basically," on, I move to strike.

THE COURT: Yes. I don't know precisely what it means.

Read the last answer to him. Try to use words that would satisfy the requirements of an answer to the question, Mr. Witness.

THE WITNESS: I can continue. As the police got right up on the demonstrators and began to club the people who were around the base of the statue, I then said as loudly as I could, "If the police want a riot, let them stay in this area. If the police don't want a riot, let them get out of this area."

MR. WEINGLASS: Did there come a time when you left the area?

THE WITNESS: Yes, I left—after I urged people to leave the area, I then left the area myself. I went back to the Mobilization office.

MR. WEINGLASS: Did you have occasion to meet with Tom Hayden that night?

THE WITNESS: Yes, I did. We went to several places and finally we went to the Conrad Hilton. I guess it was a little before midnight. Tom ran into some friends that he knew, a man named Mr. Alder, and some others. I think Jeff Cowan was present, people that I don't know very well.

And they were involved in various capacities in an official way with the Democratic Convention, and they invited Tom to come into the Conrad Hilton to watch the Convention on television. So Tom and myself then accompanied them to the entrance on Balbo Street.

MR. WEINGLASS: Were they successful in getting Tom Hayden into the hotel?

THE WITNESS: No. They returned shortly after that, and Tom said we couldn't get in.

MR. WEINGLASS: Then what did you do?

THE WITNESS: I proceeded to walk across the intersection of Balbo, going north on Michigan. Tom Hayden was directly behind, and I guess I was about halfway across the street on Balbo when I heard someone yell very loudly, "Get him, get him " screaming from a distance, and I turned around and saw the policeman who had been following me through the Convention week, Ralph Bell, running very fast, directly at Tom, and he just charged across Michigan Avenue. Tom and I were sort of frozen in our places, and Bell grabbed Tom around the neck and just drove him to the street.

At that point a second police officer in uniform came from behind and grabbed Tom as well, and I believe he actually held the nightstick against Tom's neck. I then took a few steps towards Bell and Tom and this second police officer, and I yelled at Bell, "What do you think you're doing?"

And then this uniformed policeman took his nightclub and chopped me across the neck and then twice across the chest. Then my second police tail whom I hadn't seen at that point, suddenly had me by my shirt, dragged me across the intersection of Balbo and Michigan, and just threw me up against something. I think it was a lightpole. I remember just being smashed against something, and he said—his name was Riggio—he said, "What do you think you're doing, Davis?"

MR. WEINGLASS: Were you placed under arrest at that time?

THE WITNESS: No, I was not.

MR. WEINGLASS: Did you see what happened to Tom Hayden?

THE WITNESS: Tom was put into a paddy wagon, and taken away from the area.

MR. WEINGLASS: What did you do then?

THE WITNESS: Well, I stood still for a moment, just stunned, wandered around alone, then I ran into Paul Potter. Then Paul and I walked back to the office on Dearborn Street.

MR. WEINGLASS: Now, do you recall approximately what time of night you arrived at the office?

THE WITNESS: Well, frankly I don't think that I would recall except that Mr. Riggio when he testified in this trial, indicated the arrest was around midnight, and it's about a five- or ten-minute walk back to the office, so it must have been somewhere between 12:20, 12:30 in that area.

MR. WEINGLASS: When you got back to the office, what, if anything, did you do?

THE WITNESS: Well, I called our legal defense office and explained what had occurred. Then I made a few more phone calls, talked to some people in the office. Paul left the office, and shortly after Paul left, I got in a car and drove towards Lincoln Park.

MR. WEINGLASS: Now, do you recall any of the persons who were in the office at the time you have just indicated?

THE WITNESS: Well, Paul and Carrol Glassman were both in the office, and Jeff Gerth. As a matter of fact, I think it was Jeff Gerth who drove me to Lincoln Park.

MR. WEINGLASS: Now, do you know what time it was that you left the office?

THE WITNESS: Close to one o'clock.

MR. WEINGLASS: Now, when you arrived at Lincoln Park, did you go to the park?

THE WITNESS: No, I did not go into the park. I drove past the park and into the Old Town area, and there I saw Vern Grizzard. I got out of the car and talked to Vernon for a couple of minutes and then Vernon and I got back into the car and we then left the area.

MR. WEINGLASS: Now, approximately twenty-four hours later, very late Tuesday night, do you recall where you were at that time?

THE WITNESS: Well, late Tuesday night I was in Grant Park directly across from the Conrad Hilton Hotel.

MR. WEINGLASS: Now, at 4:00 a.m., were you still in the park?

THE WITNESS: Yes. Yes, I was there certainly up till four o'clock.

MR. WEINGLASS: Did you have occasion at that time to see any of the defendants?

THE WITNESS: Yes, I met with Tom Hayden.

MR. WEINGLASS: Can you describe Tom Hayden's appearance at that time?

THE WITNESS: Well, Tom had a ridiculous hat, and he was sort of dressed in mod clothing. I think he had a fake goatee, as I recall, and for a while he was carrying a handkerchief across his nose and mouth.

I said, "Tom, you look like a fool."

MR. WEINGLASS: Did you and Tom have a conversation after that?

THE WITNESS: Yes. Yes, we did. I said to Tom that I was concerned about the lateness of the hour, I was concerned that television and cameras and photographers and newsmen were now leaving the area; the crowd was thinning out.

I said that this is the kind of situation which could lead to problems, and I told Tom that I thought that someone should make an announcement that this has been a great victory, that we're able to survive under these incredibly difficult conditions, and that people should now be encouraged to leave the park, and return tomorrow morning. Tom then agreed to make that announcement.

MR. WEINGLASS: The following morning, Wednesday, August 28, do you recall where you were?

THE WITNESS: Wednesday morning before Grant Park I was in the Mobilization office. Fifteen people, something like that, were having a meeting.

MR. WEINGLASS: Do you recall who was present at that meeting?

THE WITNESS: I recall that both Tom and Dave Dellinger were present. Linda Morse I think was there.

MR. WEINGLASS: Will you relate to the Court and jury what the defendants said while they were there, including yourself?

THE WITNESS: Dave said that he thought after the rally in Grant Park the most important thing to do was to continue with our plan to march to the Amphitheatre.

Tom said that there is no possibility of going to the Amphitheatre.

Dave said that the City, even though it has not granted permits, has allowed us to have other marches, and that perhaps they will allow us to go to the Amphitheatre.

Tom insisted that we were not going to the Amphitheatre.

Then David said that he felt that even if the police did not allow us to march, that it was absolutely necessary that we assemble, we line up, and we prepare to go to the Amphitheatre. Dave said that if the police indicate that they are going to prevent this march by force, that we have to at that time say to the world that there are Americans who will not submit to a police state by default; that they are prepared to risk arrest and be taken away to jail rather than to submit to the kind of brutality that we had seen all through the week.

Tom said that he agreed that there were people coming who intended to march, but he said as well there are many people who are not prepared to be arrested and he thought that we needed now to suggest another activity for Wednesday afternoon and evening for those people who were not prepared to be arrested.

Dave said he agreed that those people who were unprepared to be arrested should be encouraged to leave the park and return to the hotels as we had the night before.

I then said that I thought that we needed as well to announce that those people who do not want to participate in either activity should simply stay in the park or go home.

Everyone agreed with that and Dave then said that this should be announced from the platform, these three positions, and that I should inform the marshals of these three positions.

MR. WEINGLASS: Now, directing your attention to approximately 2:30 in the afternoon of that same day, do you recall where you were at that time?

THE WITNESS: Yes, I was in Grant Park just south of the refreshment stand. I saw a commotion near the flagpole and shortly after that I heard Dave Dellinger's voice. It was clear that something was happening and Dave indicated that he wanted marshals to move to the flagpole, so I then said to everyone there that we should go toward the flagpole.

MR. WEINGLASS: When you went to the flagpole, did you have anything in your hands?

THE WITNESS: I had a speaker system with a microphone.

MR. WEINGLASS: As you arrived in the vicinity of the flagpole, what was occurring?

THE WITNESS: The flag had been lowered to halfmast and the police were dragging a young man out of the area. The police seemed to be withdrawing from the area as I arrived, and a lot of people who were gathered around the flagpole began to throw anything they could get their hands on at the police who were withdrawing from the crowd. They threw rocks and boards and lunches and anything that was available right on the ground.

MR. WEINGLASS: What were you saying, if anything, at that time on the microphone?

THE WITNESS: I kept directing the marshals to form a line, link arms, and then I constantly urged the people in the crowd to stop throwing things. I said, "You're throwing things at our own people. Move back."

As our marshal line grew, I urged our marshal line to now begin to move back and move the demonstrators away from the police.

MR. WEINGLASS: Where did you go?

THE WITNESS: I continued to stand in front of the marshal line that had been formed.

MR. WEINGLASS: What did you then observe happen?

THE WITNESS: Well, at that time another squadron of policemen in formation began to advance towards my position.

I was standing in front of our marshal line sort of sandwiched in between our marshal line and the advancing police formation.

MR. WEINGLASS: What were you doing as the police were advancing?

THE WITNESS: Well, as the police advanced, I continued to have my back to the police line, basically concerned that the marshal line not break or move. Then the police formation broke and began to run, and at that time I heard several of the men in the line yell, quite distinctly, "Kill Davis! Kill Davis!" and they were screaming that and the police moved on top of me, and I was trapped between my own marshal line and advancing police line.

The first thing that occurred to me was a very powerful blow to the head that drove me face first down into the dirt, and then, as I attempted to crawl on my hands and knees, the policemen continued to yell, "Kill Davis! Kill Davis!" and continued to strike me across the ear and the neck and the back.

I guess I must have been hit thirty or forty times in the back and I crawled for maybe—I don't know how many feet, ten feet maybe, and I came to a chain fence and somehow I managed to crawl either under or through that fence, and a police fell over the fence, trying to get me, and another police hit the fence with his nightstick, but I had about a second or two in which I could stand and I leaped over a bench and over some people and into the park, and then I proceeded to walk toward the center of the park.

MR. WEINGLASS: As you walked toward the center of the park, what, if anything, happened?

THE WITNESS: Well, I guess the first thing that I was conscious of, I looked down, and my tie was just solid blood, and I realized that my shirt was just becoming blood, and someone took my arm and took me to the east side of the Bandshell, and I laid down, and there was a white coat who was bent over me. I remember hearing the voice of Carl Oglesby. Carl said, "In order to survive in this country, we have to fight," and then—then I lost consciousness.

MR. WEINGLASS: I have completed my direct examination.

THE COURT: Is there any cross-examination of this witness?

MR. FORAN: Mr. Davis, could you tell me what you consider conventional forms of protest?

THE WITNESS: Writing, speaking, marching, assembling, acting on your deepest moral and political convictions, especially when the authority that you —

MR. FORAN: I mean methods. You were going along fine.

THE WITNESS: Well, conventional activity would include those forms and others.

MR. FORAN: All right. And do you support those forms of protest or do you like other forms of protest?

THE WITNESS: It depends on what the issue is.

MR. FORAN: Haven't you stated in the past that you opposed the tendency to conventional forms of protest instead of militant action in connection with Chicago?

THE WITNESS: Well, it really depends at what time that was.

MR. FORAN: Well, in March, say.

MR. WEINGLASS: If he is referring to a prior writing, I would like him to identify it so we may follow it.

MR. FORAN: There is no necessity for me to do that, your Honor.

THE COURT: No, no necessity for that. I order the witness to answer the question if he can. If he can't he may say he cannot and I will excuse him.

Now read the question again to the witness.

THE WITNESS: I understand the question. Maybe if Mr. Foran could define for me what he means by the word "militant," because we may have different views about that word.

THE COURT: There is no necessity for defining words.

THE WITNESS: I would like very much to answer your question, Mr. Foran, but I am afraid that your view of militant and mine are very different, so I cannot answer that question as you phrased it.

THE COURT: He said he cannot answer the question, Mr. Foran. Therefore I excuse him from answering the question.

MR. FORAN: Did you tell that meeting at Lake Villa that the summer of '68 should be capped by a week of demonstrations, disruptions, and marches at the Democratic National Convention clogging the streets of Chicago?

THE WITNESS: Well, I certainly might have said "clogging the streets of Chicago."

MR. FORAN: Did you tell them at that meeting what I just said to you?

THE WITNESS: Well. I may have.

MR. FORAN: Did you ever write a document with Tom Hayden called "Discussions on the Democratic Challenge?"

THE WITNESS: Yes, I recall this. This was written very early.

MR. FORAN: When did you write it?

THE WITNESS: I think we wrote that document around January 15.

MR. FORAN: Have you ever said that "Countless creative activities must be employed that will force the President to use troops to secure his nomination?" Have you ever stated that?

THE WITNESS: That's possible.

MR. FORAN: But in January, in your little document that you and Hayden wrote together, that's what you said you were going to do, wasn't it?

THE WITNESS: Well, you've taken it out of context. I would be happy to explain the whole idea.

MR. FORAN: And it was your intention that you wanted to have trouble start so that the National Guard would have to be called out to protect the delegates, wasn't it?

THE WITNESS: No, it was not.

MR. FORAN: You've stated that, haven't you?

THE WITNESS: No. We thought it might be possible the troops would be brought into the city to protect the Convention from its own citizens, it would be another —

MR. FORAN: From the citizens that were outside waiting to pin the delegates in, is that correct?

THE WITNESS: No. It's not correct.

MR. FORAN: On August 2 you met Stahl for breakfast over at the coffee house and you told him that this was an incendiary situation and that you'd rather die right here in Chicago than in Vietnam, didn't you?

THE WITNESS: No, Mr. Foran. I don't want to die in Chicago or Vietnam.

MR. FORAN: Then you saw Stahl again on August 10, that time at the coffee shop on Monroe Street?

THE WITNESS: Yes, that's right.

MR. FORAN: And you told Stahl that you had housing for 30,000 people, didn't you?

THE WITNESS: That's right.

MR. FORAN: And you told Stahl that you expected at least another 70,000 people to come, and they wouldn't have any place to go, so they had to sleep in the park.

THE WITNESS: I think that I did.

MR. FORAN: And Stahl told you about the park ordinance again, didn't he, reminded you of it, that they couldn't sleep overnight in the park? He also told you about the Secret Service security requirements at the Amphitheater, didn't he, at the August 10 meeting?

THE WITNESS: No, no, absolutely not. On the contrary, there was no indication of a security area until August 21.

MR. FORAN: You told the City that you had to be able to march to the Amphitheatre, didn't you?

THE WITNESS: Well, I told the City that we would assemble in any area that was in proximity to the Amphitheatre.

MR. FORAN: That the terminal point of march had to be the Amphitheatre, didn't you say that?

THE WITNESS: No, I never said that. I talked about eyeshot or being near the Amphitheatre.

MR. FORAN: By the way, you people got permits at the Pentagon, didn't you?

THE WITNESS: Yes, permits were granted for the demonstration at the Pentagon.

MR. FORAN: And the Mobilization had planned or some people in it had planned civil disobedience at the Pentagon, isn't that right?

THE WITNESS: What do you mean by civil disobedience?

MR. FORAN: In fact, at the Pentagon, you planned both an active confrontation with the warmakers and the engagement of civil disobedience, didn't you?

THE WITNESS: Well, if 150,000 people gathered in assembly is regarded as an active confrontation, as I regard it, the answer, of course, is yes.

MR. FORAN: Isn't it a fact that on the August 12 meeting with Stahl that you told him that during Convention week the demonstrators were going to participate in civil disobedience? Isn't that a fact?

THE WITNESS: No. May I say what I said?

MR. FORAN: Isn't it a fact that you had found that that was a very successful tactic at the Pentagon?

THE WITNESS: No, I believe that Dave Dellinger said that that was a tactic we did not want to use in Chicago. We had one tactic for the Pentagon and another view for Chicago.

MR. FORAN: Isn't it a fact that that tactic, a permit on the one hand and active confrontation combined with civil disobedience on the other hand, gives the movement an opportunity to get both conventional protest groups and active resistance groups to come together in the demonstration? You have heard Dellinger say that, haven't you?

THE WITNESS: No, he never used those words for Chicago, Mr. Foran. What he always said—

MR. FORAN: Did he say it in connection with the Pentagon?

THE WITNESS: Oh, for the Pentagon? There was no doubt there was a conception for civil disobedience which was wholly different from what we wanted to do in Chicago. Can't you understand? It is so simple. The Pentagon was one thing, Chicago was another thing.

MR. FORAN: I know you would like to explain away what happened in Chicago very much, Mr. Davis, but you also have to take into consideration what happened at the Pentagon was the blueprint for Chicago and you know it.

MR. DELLINGER: You are a liar.

MR. KUNSTLER: Your Honor, every time we try to get one of our witnesses to talk about the Pentagon, who was the quickest on his feet to say "That is outside the scope, you can't go into that—

MR. FORAN: Not on cross-examination it isn't outside the scope.

Isn't it a fact that Mr. Dellinger said that the Mobilization at the Pentagon can have its maximum impact when it combines massive action with the cutting edge of resistance? Didn't he say that?

THE WITNESS: What do you mean "cutting edge of resistance?"

MR. FORAN: Did Mr. Dellinger ever say that?

THE WITNESS: Well, I never heard him use those words.

MR. FORAN: In substance did you hear him say it? In substance?

THE WITNESS: Yes, all right.

MR. FORAN: Isn't it a fact that your plan both at the Pentagon and in Chicago was to combine, in Dellinger's words, the peacefulness of Gandhi and the violence of active resistance? Isn't that a fact?

THE WITNESS:. No, that is not a fact. In fact, that is not even close.

MR. FORAN: May that be stricken, your Honor?

THE COURT: "In fact, that is not even close," those words may go out and the jury is directed to disregard them.

MR. FORAN: You testified on direct examination that on February 11, 1969, you gave a talk at 407 South Dearborn, didn't you?

THE WITNESS: Yes, sir.

MR. FORAN: Very good.

THE WITNESS: Thank you.

MR. FORAN: In the course of that talk you said on direct examination that "there may be people in this room who do believe that the Democratic Convention which is responsible for the war should be physically disrupted."

THE WITNESS: Yes.

MR. FORAN: Isn't it a fact that among the people in that room at 407 South Dearborn who did believe that the Democratic National Convention should be physically disrupted and torn apart were you and Hayden? Isn't that a fact?

THE WITNESS: No, it is not a fact. If you will read my testimony, you will see that—

MR. FORAN: You and Hayden had written—

THE WITNESS: Yes. Now if you will put that document before the jury.

MR. FORAN: —a "Discussion on the Democratic Convention Challenge," hadn't you?

THE WITNESS: We wrote a paper in January that was substantially revised by that very meeting, sir.

MR. FORAN: So you changed your mind between January 15 and February 11, is that your testimony?

THE WITNESS: We did not change our mind. We dropped some of the language that Dave Dellinger criticized as inappropriate, confusing—I think he said the word "disruption" was irresponsible.

MR. FORAN: In addition to you and Hayden, isn't it a fact that another person in that room who wanted to physically disrupt that National Democratic Convention was Dave Dellinger? Isn't that a fact?

THE WITNESS: Your questions embarrass me, they are so terrible. They really do.

MR. FORAN: Well, answer it.

THE WITNESS: The answer is no.

MR. FORAN: Isn't it a fact that Dellinger ran the show at the Pentagon? Isn't that a fact?

THE WITNESS: Sir, our movement doesn't work that way with one man running the show, as you say. It is a movement of thousands of people who participate each year.

MR. FORAN: You said that the Yippies wanted a gigantic festival in the park in Chicago to show the contrast between your culture and the death-producing culture of the Democratic Convention. Did you so testify?

THE WITNESS: I think I said "the death-producing ritual of the Democratic Convention."

MR. FORAN: Isn't it a fact that all the vile and vulgar propaganda the Yippies were passing out was for the purpose of making the City delay on the permit, and to make the authorities look repressive?

THE WITNESS: Sir, no one had to make the City look repressive. The City *was* repressive.

MR. FORAN: Isn't it a fact that that vile and vulgar advertising along with all of the talk about a rock festival was for the purpose of attracting the guerrilla active resistance types to your protest?

THE WITNESS: No, sir.

MR. FORAN: And the purpose of the permit negotiations was to attract people who believed in more conventional forms of protest, wasn't it?

THE WITNESS: The purpose of the permits was to allow us to have a legal assembly.

MR. FORAN: That is exactly what you had done at the Pentagon, wasn't it, the synthesis of Gandhi and guerrilla, isn't that what you did at the Pentagon?

THE WITNESS: No.

MR. FORAN: Mr. Davis, you testified that you had young Mark Simons request the use of various park facilities for meeting and for sleeping back around the thirty-first of July, isn't that correct?

THE WITNESS: Yes.

MR. FORAN: Now, isn't it a fact that you were always told by every city official that the 11:00 p.m. curfew in the parks would not be waived, isn't that a fact? Stahl told you that again on August 2, didn't he?

THE WITNESS: Not that emphatically.

MR. FORAN: He told you there was an 11:00 p.m. curfew that did not permit sleeping in the parks, did he say that?

THE WITNESS: But in the context at that time it would be waived, as it was waived all the time for the Boy Scouts and the National Guard troops.

MR. FORAN: Well, you didn't consider the Yippies Boy Scouts, did you?

THE WITNESS: Well, I considered that under the Civil Rights Act that American citizens have equal protection of the law.

MR. FORAN: You think that the Yippies with what they were advertising they were going to do in Lincoln Park are the same as the Boy Scouts? Is that what you are saying?

THE WITNESS: Well, as someone who has been very active in the Boy Scouts during all of his young life, I considered —

MR. FORAN: Did you ever see the Boy Scouts advertise public fornication, for heaven's sake?

THE WITNESS: The Yippies talked about a festival of Life and love and —

MR. FORAN: They also talked about public fornication and about drug use and about nude-ins on the beach? They also talked about that, didn't they?

THE WITNESS: They talked about love, yes, sir.

MR. FORAN: You and I have a little different feeling about love, I guess, Mr. Davis.

Now, isn't it a fact that the continuous demands for sleeping in the park were just for the purpose of again making the authorities appear repressive, isn't that a fact?

THE WITNESS: Oh, no. We wanted Soldiers Field as a substitute, or any facility. I indicated to the superintendent that we would take any facilities that could possibly be made available to get around this ordinance problem.

MR. FORAN: Now, in Judge Lynch's chambers, Raymond Simon proposed four different march routes as alternatives to your proposed march routes, didn't he?

THE WITNESS: Surely.

MR. FORAN: And you told him that while they appeared reasonable for daytime demonstrations, they were completely unacceptable to your coalition because there was no consideration of an assembly at the Amphitheater?

THE WITNESS: Yes, sir, I did.

MR. FORAN: Did you accept any of these proposals of the four routes of march?

THE WITNESS: Yes. Well, we accepted the proposal to assemble in Grant Park at 1:00 to 4:00 p.m.

MR. FORAN: And no other proposals were accepted, is that correct?

THE WITNESS: No other proposals were made.

MR. FORAN: Other proposals that Mr. Simon had made to you, you rejected, did you not? You rejected them saying that you wanted to assemble at the Amphitheatre?

THE WITNESS: They were absurd proposals. People everywhere understood why young people were coming to Chicago: to go to the Convention.

MR. FORAN: After all of these meetings, the case was argued?

THE WITNESS: On August 22, yes, sir.

MR. FORAN: And it was dismissed on the next day, August 23, is that right?

THE WITNESS: That's right, by the former law partner of Mayor Daley.

MR. FORAN: We can strike that statement.

THE COURT: I strike the remark of the witness from the record, and direct the jury to disregard it.

MR. FORAN: Was a motion to disqualify the judge made by your attorneys in this case?

THE WITNESS: No, it was not.

MR. FORAN: Did you instruct them to do so?

THE WITNESS: We discussed it as to whether or not we could get a fair shake from a former law partner of Mayor Daley, and we decided all of the judges were essentially the same, and that most of them are appointed by Daley.

MR. FORAN: So you thought all eleven judges in this district were appointed by Mayor Daley?

THE WITNESS: Not all eleven judges were sitting at that time. We thought that the court might be a face-saving device for the mayor. A mayor who didn't politically want to give permits might allow the courts to give permits. That is why we went into court.

THE COURT: Did you say all of the judges were appointed by Mayor Daley? Does he have the power to appoint judges?

THE WITNESS: No, I think that I indicated that they were all sort of very influenced and directed by the Mayor of the city of Chicago. There is a lot of feeling about it in the city.

There is a lot of feeling of that in this city, Judge Hoffman. You can't really separate the courts from the Daley machine in this town.

THE COURT: Did you know that I was just about the first judge nominated on this bench by President Eisenhower in early 1953?

THE WITNESS: I do know. I understand that. You are a Republican judge.

THE COURT: I am not a Republican judge; I am a judge of all the people. I happen to be appointed by President Eisenhower in the spring of 1953.

THE WITNESS: Yes, sir, I know that.

THE COURT: So do you want to correct your statement about Mayor Daley? If Mayor Daley had his way, he wouldn't have had me. I just want to reassure you if you feel that I am here because of Mayor Daley, I am not really.

THE WITNESS: I see.

THE COURT: Mayor Daley, as far as I am concerned, and so I am told, is a good mayor. I don't think I have ever spoken three sentences to him other than—I don't know whether I spoke to him when he was on the stand here or not. Perhaps I did direct him to answer some questions, I don't know.

MR. FORAN: When you were talking to Judge Lynch, you knew that you were going to have your people stay in the park with or without a permit, didn't you, and you didn't tell the judge that, did you?

THE WITNESS: I told the judge that we wanted to avoid violence and that was the most important thing possible.

MR. FORAN: If you wanted to avoid violence so much, did you tell the people out in the ballfield across the Balbo bridge from the Hilton Hotel that you had 30,000 housing units available and if you don't want trouble in the park, why don't you come take advantage of our housing? Did you say that in Grant Park that day?

THE WITNESS: Mr. Foran, we didn't come to Chicago to sleep.

MR. FORAN: Did you say that? Did you tell those people when you were telling them to go back to Lincoln Park that night for the Yippie Festival, did you tell them, "Don't stay in the park tonight, it might cause trouble. We have got plenty of housing available"? Did you tell them that?

THE WITNESS: We made constant references to the availability of housing through our *Ramparts* wall posters, through announcements at the movement centers. We communicated very well—

MR. FORAN: Your Honor, may I have that stricken?

THE WITNESS: —that housing was available.

MR. FORAN: Well, as you were leaving that crowd from Lincoln Park, did you ever announce over that bullhorn, "Now look, we don't want any trouble in the park tonight, so any of you people who don't have housing, just let us know. We have thirty thousand housing units available"?

Did you announce that over the bullhorn while you were conducting that march?

THE WITNESS: On that occasion, no. We had other concerns, namely the arrest of Tom Hayden and Wolfe Lowenthal. But we did make constant announcements about—

MR. FORAN: You heard Oklepek testify, did you not, and it is a fact, isn't it, that at the August 9 meeting if the demonstrators were driven from the park, they ought to move out into the Loop and tie it up and bust it up, and you told the people that at that August 9 meeting, didn't you?

THE WITNESS: That is very close, very close. What I said was that they will drive people out of the parks and people will go into the Loop.

MR. FORAN: Your Honor—

THE COURT: The answer is not responsive. Therefore I must strike it.

THE WITNESS: I heard Mr. Oklepek testify to that but it is not a fact. There was something said that he—

MR. FORAN: You did tell people at that time at that meeting that if the police kept the demonstrators in the park and they couldn't get out, that you had an easy solution for it, just riot. That's what you said, didn't you?

THE WITNESS: I have never in all my life said that to riot was an easy solution to anything, ever.

MR. FORAN: And you sat here in this courtroom and you heard Officer Bock and Dwayne Oklepek and Officer Frapolly testify to all of these things, didn't you?

THE WITNESS: I listened to your spies testify about us, yes, sir, and it was a disgrace to me.

MR. FORAN: And isn't it a fact that you structured your testimony sitting at that table—

THE WITNESS: The answer is no.

MR. FORAN: —on direct examination to appear similar to the testimony of the Government's witnesses but to differ in small essentials because you wanted to lend credibility to your testimony? That is a fact, isn't it?

THE WITNESS: It is not a fact and you know it.

MR. FORAN: May we strike that, your Honor. He whispered to the court reporter "and you know it."

THE COURT: Is that what you told the reporter at the end of your answer to the question?

THE WITNESS: No, I made that man to man to Mr. Foran.

MR. FORAN: Your Honor, a lawyer in court is unable to comment on his personal opinions concerning a witness and because of that reason I ask the jury be instructed to disregard Mr. Davis' comment because I cannot properly respond to it.

THE COURT: "And you know it," to Mr. Foran, words to that effect may go out, and the jury is directed to disregard them.

THE WITNESS: I hope after this trial you can properly respond, Mr. Foran. I really do. I hope we have that chance.

MR. FORAN: I don't know what he is—what are you—

THE WITNESS: That you and I can sit down and talk about what happened in Chicago and why it happened.

THE COURT: Mr. Witness—

THE WITNESS: I would like to do that very much.

THE COURT: Mr. Witness—

MR. FORAN: Your Honor—

THE COURT: Do you hear me, sir?

THE WITNESS: Yes, I do.

THE COURT: You didn't—

THE WITNESS: I am sorry.

THE COURT: You paid no attention to me.

I direct you not to make any volunteered observations. I have made this order several times during your testimony.

THE WITNESS: I apologize.

THE COURT: I do not accept your apology, sir.


MR. FORAN: You and your people wanted to have violence in Lincoln Park, didn't you?

THE WITNESS: No, sir. We wanted to avoid violence.

MR. FORAN: You wanted it for one purpose. You wanted it for the purpose of discrediting the Government of the United States, isn't that correct?

THE WITNESS: I wanted to discredit the Government's policies by bringing a half million Americans to Chicago at the time of the Convention.

MR. FORAN: Have you ever said that you came to Chicago to display a growing militant defiance of the authority of the government?

THE WITNESS: I don't recall saying that.

MR. FORAN: Could you have said it?

THE WITNESS: Well, that would be out of context. I would talk about the war. I would talk about racism.

MR. FORAN: Have you ever said it in context or out of context?

THE WITNESS: But the context is all-important, don't you see? It is most important.

MR. FORAN: Not in a statement like that. Have you ever said that?

THE WITNESS: Show me the document.

MR. FORAN: I am asking you a question. I want you to tell me.

THE WITNESS: I don't recall ever saying that.

MR. FORAN: And you wanted violence at the International Amphitheatre also, didn't you?

THE WITNESS: Just the opposite.

MR. FORAN: Isn't it a fact that you wanted violence in order to impose an international humiliation on the people who ruled this country? Isn't that a fact?

THE WITNESS: It is my belief that it was you wanted the violence, Mr. Foran, not me.

MR. FORAN: Your Honor, may that be stricken, and may I have the question answered?

THE COURT: Certainly, the statement may go out. The witness is directed to be careful about his answers. Please read the question for the witness.

*(question read)*

THE WITNESS: I did not want violence, Mr. Foran.

MR. FORAN: You did want to impose an international humiliation on the people who ruled this country, isn't that correct?

THE WITNESS: I am afraid that our government has already humiliated itself in the world community, sir.

MR. FORAN: Now, you had another alternative to the march to the Amphitheatre, didn't you?

THE WITNESS: Yes, sir.

MR. FORAN: And that was for people who didn't want to march to drift away in small groups from the Bandshell and return to the hotel areas in the Loop.

THE WITNESS: That is right.

MR. FORAN: And it was planned, wasn't it, that they were to come back to the Hilton Hotel in force and cause a violent confrontation with the police, wasn't it?

THE WITNESS: No, of course not.

MR. FORAN: Was the objective of the second alternative to paralyze the "magnificent mile" of Michigan Avenue?

THE WITNESS: No, that is a Government theory, a Government theory to try to figure out and explain away what happened in Chicago.

MR. FORAN: You have actually stated, haven't you, that all of those things I have been asking you about were the things that you accomplished in Chicago, haven't you?

THE WITNESS: You mean violent confrontations and tearing up the city and—

MR. FORAN: That the purpose of your meeting in Chicago was to impose an international humiliation on the people who rule this country, to display a growing militant defiance of the authority of the Government, to paralyze the "magnificent mile" of Michigan Avenue. You have said all of those things, haven't you, that that was your purpose in coming to Chicago and that you achieved it?

THE WITNESS: No, I never indicated that that was our purpose in coming to Chicago.

MR. FORAN: Did you ever write a document, coauthor one with Tom Hayden, called "Politics After Chicago?"

THE WITNESS: I may have.

MR. FORAN: I show you Government's Exhibit No. 104 for identification and ask you if that is a copy of it.

THE WITNESS: Yes. You have butchered the context, just as I suspected.

MR. FORAN: Now, have you and Mr. Hayden stated in this "Politics After Chicago" that since the institutions of this country cannot be changed from within, the people will take to the streets? Have you stated that?

THE WITNESS: Yes. I wish you would read the whole context.

MR. FORAN: You have stated that, have you not?

THE WITNESS: Yes.

MR. FORAN: You have stated "We learned in Chicago what it means to declare that the streets belong to the people."

THE WITNESS: Yes.

MR. FORAN: Did you state that the battle line is no longer drawn in the obscure paddies of Vietnam or the dim ghetto streets, but is coming closer to suburban sanctuaries and corporate board rooms? The gas that fell on us in Chicago also fell on Hubert? The street that was paralyzed was the "magnificent mile" of Michigan Avenue?

THE WITNESS: Yes. That is quite different from what you said before.

MR. FORAN: Did you state this:

"Our strategic purpose is two-fold: To display a growing militant defiance of the authority of the Government."

Did you state that?

THE WITNESS: It is possible. Read the whole document.

MR. FORAN: You stated that, didn't you?

THE WITNESS: Why don't you read the whole document or give it to the jury?

MR. FORAN: You have stated that your program is to discredit the authority of the Government which is deaf to its own system and railroad an election through America as if Vietnam were the caboose?

THE WITNESS: Boy, that's right on.

MR. FORAN: You stated that, did you not, that you wanted to discredit the authority of a Government which is deaf to its own citizens?

THE WITNESS: Well, I embrace those words. I don't know if I said them, but those words are just right.

MR. FORAN: And you believe that you won what you called the Battle of Chicago, don't you?

THE WITNESS: What do you mean by the Battle of Chicago?

MR. FORAN: Have you ever called what occurred in Chicago during the Convention the Battle of Chicago?

THE WITNESS: Yes, and I have defined it and I wonder if you would let me define it here. I will be happy to answer the question.

MR. FORAN: Have you ever stated in the words that I have asked you, "We won the Battle of Chicago"? Have you ever said that in any context?

THE WITNESS: You are not interested in the context, I suppose.

MR. FORAN: In any context, Mr. Davis.

THE WITNESS: Yes, I believe we won the battle in Chicago.

MR. FORAN: That you—it was your—your program would include press conferences, disruptions and pickets dramatizing whatever demands you wanted?

THE WITNESS: May I see the context so we can clarify it?

MR. FORAN: I show you Government's Exhibit No. 99. It starts at the top.

THE WITNESS: Yes. I was right.

MR. FORAN: Now, you feel that the Battle of Chicago continues, don't you?

THE WITNESS: Yes, I believe that contest that will shape the political character  in the next decade was really shaped in Chicago in the context between the Daleys and the Nixons, and the Hayakawas, and the Reagans and the young people who expressed their hopes in the streets in Chicago. And I think, frankly, in that context, it is going to be clear it is not the Daleys, or the Humphreys, or the Johnsons who are the future of this country. We are the future of this country.

MR. FORAN: Isn't it a fact that you have said, Mr. Davis, that the Battle of Chicago continues today. The war is on. The reason we are here tonight is to try to figure out how we are going to get the kind of mutiny that Company A started in South Vietnam and spread it to every army base, every high school, every community in this country. That is what you said about the Battle of Chicago continuing today, isn't it?

THE WITNESS: Young people in South Vietnam—

MR. FORAN: Haven't you said just exactly what I read to you, sir?

MR. WEINGLASS: Your Honor, could we have the date of that statement?

THE COURT: Certainly, if you have the date, give it to him.

THE WITNESS: August 28, 1969.

MR. FORAN: On the one year anniversary of what happened on Wednesday, August 28, 1968?

THE WITNESS: A year after the Convention.

MR. FORAN: Isn't it a fact that you have said, "If we go about our own work, and if we make it clear that there can be no peace in the United States until every soldier is brought out of Vietnam and this imperialistic system is destroyed." Have you said that?

THE WITNESS: I don't recall those exact words, but those certainly are my sentiments, that we should not rest until this war is over and until the system—

MR. FORAN: And until this imperialistic system is destroyed?

THE WITNESS: Until the system that made that war is changed, the foreign policy.

MR. FORAN: The way you decided to continue the Battle of Chicago, the way you decided to fight the Battle of Chicago, was by incitement to riot, wasn't it?

THE WITNESS: No, sir, by organizing, by organizing within the army, within high schools, within factories and communities across this country.

MR. FORAN: By inciting to riot within high schools, and within colleges, and within factories, and within the army, isn't that right, sir?

THE WITNESS: No. No, sir. No, I am trying to find a way that this generation can make this country something better than what it has been.

MR. FORAN: Your Honor, he is no longer responding to the question.

THE COURT: I strike the answer of the witness and direct the jury to disregard it.

MR. FORAN: And what you want to urge young people to do is to revolt, isn't that right?

THE WITNESS: Yes, revolt.

MR. FORAN: And you have stated, have you not, "That there can be no question by the time that I am through that I have every intention of urging that you revolt, that you join the Movement, that you become a part of a growing force for insurrection in the United States". You have said that, haven't you?

THE WITNESS: I was standing right next to Fred Hampton when I said that, who was murdered in this city by policemen.

MR. FORAN: Your Honor, I move to strike that.

THE COURT: Yes, the answer may certainly go out. The question is wholly unrelated to one Fred Hampton.

MR. FORAN: Wouldn't it be wonderful, your Honor, if the United States accused people of murder as these people do without proof, without trial, and without any kind of evidence having been presented in any kind of a decent situation.

MR. KUNSTLER: A man is murdered in his bed, while he is sleeping, by the police.

MR. FORAN: With nineteen guns there.

THE COURT: I am trying this case. I will ask you, Mr. Kunstler, to make no reference to that case because it is not in issue here.

MR. FORAN: In Downers Grove on August 30, you told all of the people out there, "We have won America." Didn't you tell them that? Didn't you tell them that?

THE WITNESS: I believe that I said —

MR. FORAN: Didn't you say that to them out at Downers Grove, sir?

THE WITNESS: Yes, sir, I did.

MR. FORAN: I have no further cross-examination.

THE COURT: Redirect examination.

MR. WEINGLASS: Redirect is unnecessary, your Honor.

# Testimony Of Bobby Seale

MR. KUNSTLER: Would you state your full name?

THE WITNESS: Bobby G. Seale.

MR. KUNSTLER: And, Mr. Seale, what is your occupation?

THE WITNESS: Presently, I am the Chairman of the Black Panther Party.

MR. KUNSTLER: Would you state what is the Black Panther Party for Self-Defense?

THE WITNESS: The Black Panther Party —

MR. SCHULTZ: Objection.

THE COURT: I sustain the objection.

MR. KUNSTLER: Your Honor, every single witness on the stand called by the defense has been entitled to tell what is the organization in which his occupation pertained.

MR. SCHULTZ: We are not litigating the Black Panther Party, your Honor, in this case.

THE COURT: I will let my ruling stand, sir.

MR. KUNSTLER: Mr. Seale, would you state for the Court and jury what your duties are as Chairman of the Black Panther Party?

THE WITNESS: As the Chairman of the Black Panther Party, I am a member of the central committee who have to make speaking engagements, representing the Party's program, the Party's ideology, the social programs that we are setting forth in communities to deal with political, economic, and social evils and injustices that exist in this American society.

I go on a number of speaking engagements. I do quite a bit of coordinating work and direct community organizing in the black community and relate to other organizations whom we have coalitions with. We form alliances and direct these alliances in the same manner that brother Fred Hampton used to do before he was murdered, and we form these alliances with the Young Lords, Puerto Ricans, and also Latino people who are oppressed in America.

MR. KUNSTLER: Mr. Seale, you mentioned the name of Fred Hampton. Who was Fred Hampton?

THE WITNESS: Deputy Chairman—

MR. SCHULTZ: Objection.

THE COURT: I sustain the objection.

MR. SCHULTZ: Your Honor, if you will instruct Mr. Seale that when an objection is pending, he should wait before he answers the question—

THE COURT: Mr. Seale, when an objection is made by the opposing lawyers sitting at that table, wait until the Court decides the objection before you answer, please.

THE WITNESS: Well, should I just give a few seconds to see if there is going to be an objection?

THE COURT: Yes. Wait. It is a good idea.

THE WITNESS: Just to see if there is going to be an objection.

MR. SCHULTZ: I will try to be prompt, your Honor.

MR. KUNSTLER: Mr. Seale, I call your attention to August 27, 1968. Did there come a time when you went to the San Francisco International Airport?

THE WITNESS: Tuesday. That Tuesday in August. It was a Tuesday, I think.

MR. KUNSTLER: Did you then board an airplane?

THE WITNESS: Yes.

MR. KUNSTLER: Do you know the destination of that airplane?

THE WITNESS: Chicago, Illinois.

MR. KUNSTLER: I will ask you now to look at the defense table and I want to ask you this question whether, prior to boarding that airplane, you had ever known Jerry Rubin.

THE WITNESS: No, I had not.

MR. KUNSTLER: David Dellinger?

THE WITNESS: I never seen him before in my life.

MR. KUNSTLER: Abbie Hoffman?

THE WITNESS: I never seen him before in my life before that.

MR. KUNSTLER: Lee Weiner?

THE WITNESS: I never seen him before in my life.

MR. KUNSTLER: Rennie Davis?

THE WITNESS: I never seen him before in my life.

MR. KUNSTLER: Tom Hayden?

THE WITNESS: I had heard of his name but I had never met him or seen him before in my life.

MR. KUNSTLER: John Froines?

THE WITNESS: I never seen him or heard of him before in my life.

MR. KUNSTLER: Can you state to the Court the purpose of your trip to Chicago?

MR. SCHULTZ: Objection, your Honor.

THE COURT: I sustain the objection.

MR. KUNSTLER: Now after you arrived in Chicago on the twenty-seventh of August, did you have occasion at any time later that day to go to Lincoln Park?

THE WITNESS: Yes, it was late in the afternoon.

MR. KUNSTLER: Now when you arrived at Lincoln Park, can you recollect what was going on in the area you went to?

THE WITNESS: The area in the park that I observed was completely occupied by policemen.

The park was generally surrounded by policemen, cops everywhere, and many of those who I looked at and observed to be what I would call or define as pigs. This is what I observed, this is the impression, the facts that existed and what I saw. It was just the cops, and I myself defined it as pigs, were piggyback. This is the general way we talk in the ghetto in expressing a lot of these things.

MR. KUNSTLER: Now did there come a time, Mr. Seale, when you spoke in Lincoln Park that afternoon?

THE WITNESS: Yes, there did come a time when I did speak.

MR. KUNSTLER: I show you D-350 for identification, do you think that you could identify for us what it is?

THE WITNESS: This is a transcript from a tape recording of the speech I made there.

MR. KUNSTLER: I will show you 350-B. Is that the tape from which 350 was made?

THE WITNESS: Yes, I can recognize it.

MR. KUNSTLER: Is that tape a fair and accurate reproduction of your speech as you gave it on the afternoon of August 27 in Lincoln Park.

THE WITNESS: Yes, it is, except for the fact that the very first line, about half of the sentence on that tape, the very first line of the first sentence that I pronounced in that speech is not on that tape.

MR. KUNSTLER: With the exception of those first three or four words, it is a fair and accurate representation of the speech?

THE WITNESS: Yes.

MR. KUNSTLER: Then I would offer it into evidence.

MR. SCHULTZ: No objection.

MR. KUNSTLER: Your Honor, before this is played we will furnish to the court reporter, to save her hands, a copy of the speech.

MR. SCHULTZ: No objection.

*(tape played)*

*We've come out to speak to some people who're involved, maybe emotionally and maybe in many respects, in a drastic situation of a developing revolution. The revolution in this country at the time is in* fact the people coming forth to demand freedom. The revolution at this time is directly connected with organized guns and force.

We must understand that as we go forth to try and move the scurvy, reprobative pigs: the lynching Lyndon Baines Johnsons, the fat pig Humphreys, the jive double-lip-talkin' Nixons, the slick talkin' McCarthys — these murdering and brutalizing and oppressing people all over the world — when we go forth to deal with them — that they're gonna always send out their racist, scurvy rotten pigs to occupy the people, to occupy the community, just the way they have this park here occupied.

You know the Minister of Information, Eldridge Cleaver, who's been nominated as the Presidential candidate, Black Panther candidate, running on the Peace and Freedom ticket. As you know, the brother always says, "All power to the People." Now just a second here. You must understand what power is. The Minister of Defense, Huey P. Newton, explains and teaches that power is the ability to defend phenomena and make it act in a desired manner.

What phenomena are we talking about? We're talking about the racist, brutal murders that pigs have committed upon black people. We're talking about lynchings that's been going down for four hundred years on black people's heads. We're talking about the occupation troops, right here in Chicago, occupying the black community and even occupying this park where the people have come forth. The phenomenal situation is this: it's that we have too many hogs in every facet of government that exists in this country. We can define that.

But we said the ability to define this social phenomena and also the ability to make it act in a desired manner. How do you make the social phenomena act in a desired manner? I am saying this here, I'm pretty sure you're quite well aware of how you make it act in a desired manner. If a pig comes up to you and you sit down and start talking about slidin' in, rollin' in, jumpin' in, bugalooin' in, dancin' in, swimmin' in, prayin' in and singing "We Shall Overcome," like a lot of these Toms want us to do — we're jivin'. But if a pig comes up to us and starts swinging a billy club, and you check around and you got your piece — you gotta down that pig in defense of yourself. You gonna take that club, whip him over his head, lay him out on the ground and then this pig is acting in a desired manner. All right.

*At the same time, many individuals, many groups will run into situations where the pigs are going to attack. Always. Because the pigs have been sent here by the top hog who gave him orders from the power structure to attack the people.*

*Now listen here. If you gonna get down to nitty-gritty, brothers and people, and you don't intend to miss no nits and no grits, you got to have some functional organization to not only make one individual pig or a number of pigs act in the desired manner but to make this whole racist, decadent power structure act in a desired manner.*

*The Black Panther Party went forth when brother Huey P. Newton was busted October the 28. He was charged with making a couple of pigs act in a desired manner. And from there, a coalition between the Peace and Freedom Party, a predominately white group, and the Black Panther Party, a black organization, a revolutionary organization, formed this coalition based on the fact that the white people said they were concerned by the fact that their racist power structure in Oakland in California was going to try to railroad Huey P. Newton to the gas chamber and kill him.*

*Now this coalition developed into a more functional thing: the Peace and Freedom Party in the white community trying to end the decadent racism, the Black Panthers in the black community trying to convince us we've got to defend ourselves, liberate ourselves from the oppressed conditions that are caused by racism. This coalition has gone forth. We think it's a very functional coalition.*

*So it's very important that we understand the need for organization, cause that's what we deal with. We're not here to be sitting around a jive table vacillating and jiving ourselves. Too many times in the past, the people sit down around tables. When they sit down around these tables they get to arguing about whether or not this white racist wall that black people are chained against is real or not. They want to come talking about some molecular structure of the wall. And the molecular structure of the wall shows that wall is really ninety percent space. So is the white racist wall that we're talking about real or not? We're saying that it's here. You're damned right it's real. Because we're chained against this wall.*

*And we say this here: don't be out there jiving, wondering whether the wall is real or not. Make sure if you want to coalesce, work, functionally organize, that you pick up a crowbar. Pick up a piece.*

*Pick up a gun. And pull that spike out from the wall. Because if you pull it on out and if you shoot well, all I'm gonna do is pat you on the back and say "Keep shooting." You dig? We won't be jiving.*

*Now, there are many kinds of guns. Many, many kinds of guns. But the strongest weapon that we have, the strongest weapon that we all each individually have, is all of us. United in opposition. United with revolutionary principles.*

*So it's very necessary for us to understand the need for functional organization. It's very necessary for us, especially black brothers — listen close — that we have revolutionary principles to guide ourselves by. Because if we just go out in a jive gang, running around in big groups, with rocks and bottles, we're not going to do nothing against 500 pigs with shotguns and .357 Magnums.*

*What we got to do is functionally put ourselves in organizations. Get every black man in the black community with a shotgun in his home, and a .357 Magnum, and a .45 if he can get it, and an M-1 if he can get it and anything else if he can get it, brothers. Get it and start doing this.*

*Then, I want to say this here. On the streets, stop running in large groups. That ain't no right tactic. We should run in groups of fours and fives — all around. We cannot continue using these tactics where we lose 3000 arrested or we lose 1 or 200 dead. We gotta stop. So we want to start running in threes, fours, and fives.*

*Small groups using proper revolutionary tactics. So we can dissemble those pigs who occupy our community, who occupy our community like foreign troops.*

*Black people, we're saying we're lost. We seem to be lost in a world of white racist, decadent America. I'm saying that we have a right to defend ourselves as human beings. And if some pig comes up to us unjustly treating us injustly, then we have to bring our pieces out and start barbecuing some of that pork.*

*Brother Huey P. Newton was on the stand yesterday. And they said the brother was so beautiful in cross-examination for a whole day-and-a-half that the jury got mad at the D.A. We hope that brother Huey P. Newton be set free. We go further in our hopes, in our work in our organization to demand that he be set free.*

*And we say that if anything happens to Huey P. Newton, the sky is the limit.*

*Now here are some buckets around and we are here, Huey needs funds, and we hope that you will donate to the Party and other local organizations.*

*We hope, we sure that you can begin to set up a few things organizationally to deal with the situation in a very revolutionary manner.*

*So, Power to the People. Power to All the People. Black Power to Black People. Panther Power. Even some Peace and Freedom Power. Power and Free Huey. Thank you.*

*(end of tape)*

MR. KUNSTLER: Now, Mr. Seale, when you used the term "pig" in that speech, can you define what is meant by the word "pig"?

THE WITNESS: A pig is a person or a policeman who is generally found violating the constitutional rights and the human rights of people, a vile traducer, and he is usually found masquerading as a victim of unprovoked attack.

MR. KUNSTLER: And you also used the term in discussing Huey P. Newton "the sky is the limit." Would you explain what you meant by that?

THE WITNESS: I meant by that that we would exhaust all political and legal means through the courts all the way to the top of the Supreme Court. We would have demonstrations. We will organize the people in together and we will go to the limit to try and get our Minister of Defense free if he is not set free.

MR. KUNSTLER: I have no further question.

THE COURT: Is there any cross-examination?

MR. SCHULTZ: Yes, sir, your Honor, I have some.

Now you said in your speech that was just played before the jury that Huey P. Newton was busted and charged with making a couple of pigs act in a desired manner, did you not, Sir?

THE WITNESS: He was charged with shooting a policeman. He was charged with shooting in defense of himself.

MR. SCHULTZ: So when you said that "individuals should make pigs act in a desired manner," you were referring to shooting policemen in defense if necessary, isn't that right?

THE WITNESS: Organizationally and functionally, if you look at the whole context of the sentence, what I mean is not what you are inferring.

What I mean is this here—

MR. SCHULTZ: I am asking you what you said, sir. I am asking you, did you not state that?

THE WITNESS: But you also asked me what I mean, Mr. Schultz.

MR. KUNSTLER: I thought he asked him what he meant, too, Your Honor.

MR. SCHULTZ: Let me rephrase the question if I did.

When you stated to the people in Lincoln Park that " they've got to make one individual pig or a number of individual pigs act in the desired manner," you weren't referring to that same desired manner for which Huey Newton was charged, were you?

THE WITNESS: What was that? Rephrase your question again. I am trying to make sure you don't trip me.

MR. SCHULTZ: It was a little complicated, Mr. Seale. It wasn't very well stated.

THE WITNESS: All right.

MR. SCHULTZ: I will ask it to you again.

You said to the people, "They should make one pig or a number of pigs act in the desired manner." You were not then referring to the same desired manner with which Mr. Newton was charged, that is, shooting a policeman? Were you or were you not?

THE WITNESS: No. I can state it in another way in answering the question.

MR. SCHULTZ: No.

THE WITNESS: If you will let me answer the question.

MR. SCHULTZ: You said you were not.

THE WITNESS: Can I answer the question?

THE COURT: You have answered the question. Ask him another question.

MR. SCHULTZ: Were you referring to shooting policemen in the desired manner when you said this: "But if a pig comes up to us and starts swinging a billy club, you're gonna take that club and whip him over the head, and lay him on the ground, and then the pig is acting in a desired manner."

THE WITNESS: I was referring to defending myself.

MR. SCHULTZ: Now you said to the people, did you not, that they should pull the spike from the wall, because "if you pull it out and if you shoot well, all I am going to do is pat you on the back and say 'Keep on shooting'?" Was that for the purpose of making the pig act in the desired manner?

THE WITNESS: That's for the purpose of telling people they have to defend themselves. In that broad sense of that statement, without taking it out of context, that generally means that, and if any individual is unjustly attacked by any policeman, unjustly, at that point he has a human right—

MR. SCHULTZ: To kill the policeman.

THE WITNESS: To defend himself.

MR. SCHULTZ: And that means if necessary to kill that policeman, does it not?

THE WITNESS: If that policeman is attacking me, if he is violating the law, if he is violating the law unjustly, attacking me—I am not talking about a policeman down the street stopping somebody—

MR. SCHULTZ: That means killing, if necessary, doesn't it?

THE WITNESS: No.

MR. SCHULTZ: You will not kill a policeman, is that right?

THE WITNESS: It is not the desire to kill, and that's what you are trying to put in the tone of it, and it's not that—

MR. SCHULTZ: Will you answer my question?

THE WITNESS: I won't answer that question with a yes or no, your Honor. I have to answer the question my own way.

MR. SCHULTZ: I can rephrase it. Were you referring to shooting pigs?

THE WITNESS: I was referring to shooting any racist, bigoted pig who unjustly attacks us or brutalizes us in the process of us doing any kind of organizational and functional work to try to change the power structure and remove the oppression.

MR. SCHULTZ: And you said in that context "unjustly attacking you?"

THE WITNESS: In the context of the whole speech, that's what I am talking about.

MR. SCHULTZ: So when you told the people that what we have to do is get every black man in the black community with a shotgun in his home and a .357 Magnum and a .45, if he can get it, and an M-1, if he can get it — you were referring to getting guns for defense, isn't that right?

THE WITNESS: Getting a gun, put a gun in your home, a shotgun.

MR. SCHULTZ: In defense?

THE WITNESS: —or M-1 —you have a right by the Second Amendment of the Constitution to have it.

MR. SCHULTZ: Were you referring to it in self-defense, that is my question, sir?

THE WITNESS: I was referring to it in self-defense against unjust brutal attack by any policeman or pigs or bigots in this society who will attack people.

MR. SCHULTZ: And you said to the people in Lincoln Park "I am referring to unjust brutal attack," didn't you?

THE WITNESS: No. You know what I mean, Mr. Schultz. I am telling you what I am referring to.

MR. SCHULTZ: Now, when you told the people to stop running around in big groups and with rocks and bottles because you can't do anything against 500 pigs with shotguns, and .357 Magnums, was that part of your revolutionary tactics?

THE WITNESS: Definitely. It is a change. Revolution means change, change away from this old erroneous method of running out in the streets in big numbers and rioting, and throwing rocks and bottles. How are you going to stop a .357 Magnum or shotgun full of some shotgun shells that are being shot at you with rocks and bottles. Stop that. Stop it. Stop the rioting. That is in essence what I am talking about.

Stop those kind of tactics. Use revolutionary tactics. Defend yourself from unjust attacks, et cetera.

MR. SCHULTZ: When you told the people in Lincoln Park, "Pick up a gun, pull the spike from the wall, because if you pull it out and you shoot well, all I'm gonna do is pat you on the back and say, 'Keep on shooting,' " That was part of your revolutionary tactics too, was it not, sir?

THE WITNESS: Yes, sir, and if you look generally —

MR. SCHULTZ: Please, that is all.

THE COURT: You have answered the question.

THE WITNESS: I strike that answer on the grounds that that particular question is wrong because it ain't clear.

THE COURT: I have some news for you, sir.

*(there is applause in the courtroom)*

THE COURT: I do the striking here, and will the marshals exclude from the courtroom anyone who applauded. This isn't a theater. Anyone who applauded the witness may go out and is directed to leave.

MR. SCHULTZ: Mr. Seale, are you the Bobby G. Seale who was convicted on April 11, 1968, of being in possession of a shotgun in the vicinity of a jail?

THE WITNESS: Yes, I am the same person who was convicted later of being in possession of a shotgun as they charged me of being adjacent to a jail, but as I know by the law, you could have a shotgun as long as it wasn't concealed and as long as you are in a public place, and I was actually in fact on a public sidewalk.

Yes, I was convicted, and the thing was appealed.

MR. SCHULTZ: You had five shotgun shells in that gun, did you not?

THE WITNESS: Yes, in a magazine.

MR. SCHULTZ: Now, Mr. Seale, on Wednesday morning, you gave the second speech, right?

THE WITNESS: I guess that was Wednesday morning, in the middle of the week somewhere.

MR. SCHULTZ: And you said to the people, Mr. Seale, "If the pigs get in the way of our march, then tangle with the blue-helmeted motherfuckers. Kill them and send them to the morgue slab," and you were pointing to policemen at that time, isn't that a fact?

MR. KUNSTLER: This is completely out of the scope of the direct examination, your Honor. It is improper and it is wrong,

THE COURT: No, the witness was brought here to testify about his activities during that period. I think the Government has the right to inquire. Treating your remarks as objection which you have not made, I overrule the objection.

MR. KUNSTLER: Is your Honor ruling that every witness that takes the stand can be cross-examined on anything?

THE COURT: I said it is my ruling, sir, that that question is a proper one on this record.

MR. SCHULTZ: How many people were you speaking to?

THE WITNESS: Let's see now —

MR. GARRY: Just a minute, Mr. Seale. I am rising to the part that your Honor has heretofore allowed me to. Unless we can be given a full transcription of the speech that he gave on that day, I am going to instruct the witness not to answer the question upon the grounds of the Fifth Amendment.

THE COURT: If you so advise him and the witness wants to do it in a proper manner, I will respect his refusal to answer.

MR. GARRY: Mr. Seale, you are entitled and I advise you not to answer this question upon the ground it would tend to incriminate you under the Fifth Amendment of the United States Constitution. I so advise you to take that advice.

THE COURT: Mr. Seale, you have heard Mr. Garry. If you wish to take advantage of the Fifth Amendment and say to the Court that to answer that question might tend to incriminate you, you may do it, but it must come from you, not from your lawyer.

THE WITNESS: I would like to take the Fifth Amendment on the question, yes, sir.

THE COURT: All right. You needn't answer the question.

MR. SCHULTZ: That is all, your Honor.

THE COURT: Is there any redirect examination?

MR. KUNSTLER: Yes, your Honor.

Mr. Seale, with reference to Mr. Schultz' question regarding the conviction for carrying a shotgun, did you ever go to jail for that?

THE WITNESS: No.

MR. SCHULTZ: Objection, your Honor. That is not proper.

THE COURT: I sustain the objection. The test is the conviction, not the punishment.

MR. KUNSTLER: Mr. Seale, do you recall Mr. Schultz asked you about certain guns?

THE WITNESS: Yes, I do.

MR. KUNSTLER: Now I ask you this question. When you were referring to those guns, did you not use the phrase "in his home"?

THE WITNESS: Yes.

MR. SCHULTZ: Objection to the form of question. Mr. Kunstler is doing the testifying and using the witness as a sounding board.

THE COURT: Yes, the form is bad. I sustain the objection.

MR. KUNSTLER: All right. What did you say in that speech, Mr. Seale, with reference to where those guns were to be?

THE WITNESS: I said "Put the guns in your home, .357 Magnum, M-1, .45s." I referred to these kind of guns or anything else. You have a right to do it, and that's part of our program in the Party, a constitutional right to arm yourself.

THE COURT: All right. You've answered the question.

MR. KUNSTLER: Now, Mr. Seale, as to the speech that you gave in Lincoln Park on August 27, 1968, what type of person was this speech addressed to?

MR. SCHULTZ: Objection. I asked him nothing about the audience.

THE COURT: I sustain the objection to the question.

MR. KUNSTLER: In the light of that ruling, Your Honor, I have no further questions.

THE COURT: I have sustained the objection.

MR. SCHULTZ: I have no questions.

THE COURT: You may go. Call your next witness, please.

VOICES: Power to the people! Power to the people!

# *Testimony Of Philip David Ochs*

MR. KUNSTLER: Will you state your full name, please?

THE WITNESS: Philip David Ochs.

MR. KUNSTLER: What is your occupation?

THE WITNESS: I am a singer, a folksinger.

MR. KUNSTLER: Now, Mr. Ochs, can you indicate what kind of songs you sing?

THE WITNESS: I write all my own songs and they are just simple melodies with a lot of lyrics. They usually have to do with current events and what is going on in the news. You can call them topical songs, songs about the news, and then developing into more philosophical songs later.

MR. KUNSTLER: Now, Mr. Ochs, did there ever come a time when you met any of the defendants at this table?

THE WITNESS: Yes. I met Jerry Rubin in 1964 when he was organizing one of the first teach-ins against the war in Vietnam in Berkeley. He called me up. He asked me to come and sing.

MR. KUNSTLER: Now did you have any occasion after that to receive another such call from Mr. Rubin?

THE WITNESS: I met him a few times later in regard to other political actions. I met him in Washington at the march they had at the Pentagon incident, at the big rally before the Pentagon
.

MR. KUNSTLER: Now, Mr. Ochs, have you ever been associated with what is called the Youth International Party, or, as we will say, the Yippies?

THE WITNESS: Yes. I helped design the party, formulate the idea of what Yippie was going to be, in the early part of 1968.

MR. KUNSTLER: Can you indicate to the Court and jury what Yippie was going to be, what its purpose was for its formation?

THE WITNESS: The idea of Yippie was to be a form of theater politics, theatrically dealing with what seemed to be an increasingly absurd world and trying to deal with it in other than just on a straight moral level. They wanted to be able to act out fantasies in the street to communicate their feelings to the public.

MR. KUNSTLER: Now, were any of the defendants at the table involved in the formation of the Yippies?

THE WITNESS: Yes, Jerry Rubin and Abbie Hoffman.

MR. KUNSTLER: Can you just point to and identify which one is Jerry Rubin and which one is Abbie Hoffman?

THE WITNESS: Yes, Jerry Rubin with the headband and Abbie Hoffman with the smile.

MR. KUNSTLER: Can you indicate in general to the Court and jury what the plans were for the Yippies in Chicago during the Democratic National Convention?

THE WITNESS: The plans were essentially —

MR. FORAN: I object.

THE COURT: I sustain the objection.

MR. KUNSTLER: Your Honor, one of the central roles in this case is the Yippie participation around the Democratic National Convention.

THE COURT: I don't see that allegation in the indictment.

MR. KUNSTLER: Well, the indictment charges these two men with certain acts in connection with the Democratic National Convention.

THE COURT: These two men and others, but not as Yippies, so-called, but—as individuals.

MR. KUNSTLER: All right, your Honor, I will rephrase the question. Did there come a time when Jerry and Abbie discussed their plans?

THE WITNESS: Yes, they did, around the middle of January at Jerry's. Present there, besides Abbie and Jerry, I believe, was Paul Krassner and Ed Sanders. Tim Leary was there at one point.

MR. KUNSTLER: Can you tell the conversation from Jerry and Abbie, as to their plans in coming to Chicago around the Democratic National Convention?

THE WITNESS: OK. Jerry Rubin planned to have a Festival of Life during the National Convention, basically representing an alternate culture. They would theoretically sort of spoof the Convention and show the public, the media, that the Convention was not to be taken seriously because it wasn't fair, and wasn't going to be honest, and wasn't going to be a democratic convention. They discussed getting permits. They discussed flying to Chicago to talk with Mayor Daley. They several times mentioned they wanted to avoid violence. They went out of their way on many different occasions to talk with the Mayor or anybody who could help them avoid violence—

MR. KUNSTLER: Now, Mr. Ochs, do you know what guerrilla theater is?

THE WITNESS: Guerrilla theater creates theatrical metaphors for what is going on in the world outside.

For example, a guerrilla theater might do, let us say, a skit on the Viet Cong, it might act out a scene on a public street or in a public park where some actually play the Viet Cong, some actually play American soldiers, and they will dramatize an event, basically create a metaphor, an image, usually involving humor, usually involving a dramatic scene, and usually very short. This isn't a play with the theme built up. It's just short skits, essentially.

MR. KUNSTLER: Did Jerry Rubin or Abbie Hoffman ask you to do anything at any time?

MR. FORAN: I object to that.

THE COURT: I sustain the objection.

MR. FORAN: I object to it as leading and suggestive.

MR. KUNSTLER: Did you have any discussion with Abbie and Jerry about your role?

THE WITNESS: Yes. In early February at Abbie's apartment.

MR. KUNSTLER: Can you state what Abbie Hoffman and Jerry Rubin said to you and what you said to them?

THE WITNESS: They discussed my singing at the Festival of Life. They asked me to contact other performers to come and sing at the Festival. I talked to Paul Simon of Simon and Garfunkel. I believe I talked with Judy Collins.

MR. KUNSTLER: Did there come a time, Mr. Ochs, when you came to Chicago in 1968?

THE WITNESS: I came campaigning for Eugene McCarthy on M-Day, which I believe was August 15, at the Lindy Opera House, I believe.

MR. KUNSTLER: After you arrived in Chicago did you have any discussion with Jerry?

---

THE WITNESS: Yes, I did. We discussed the nomination of a pig for President.

MR. KUNSTLER: Would you state what you said and what Jerry said.

THE WITNESS: We discussed the details. We discussed going out to the countryside around Chicago and buying a pig from a farmer and bringing him into the city for the purposes of his nominating speech.

MR. KUNSTLER: Did you have any role yourself in that?

THE WITNESS: Yes, I helped select the pig, and I paid for him.

MR. KUNSTLER: Now, did you find a pig at once when you went out?

THE WITNESS: No, it was very difficult. We stopped at several farms and asked where the pigs were.

MR. KUNSTLER: None of the farmers referred you to the police station, did they?

THE WITNESS: No.

MR. FORAN: Objection.

THE COURT: I sustain the objection.

MR. KUNSTLER: Mr. Ochs, can you describe the pig which was finally bought?

MR. FORAN: Objection.

THE COURT: I sustain the objection.

MR. KUNSTLER: Would you state what, if anything, happened to the pig?

THE WITNESS: The pig was arrested with seven people.

MR. KUNSTLER: When did that take place?

THE WITNESS: This took place on the morning of August 23, at the Civic Center underneath the Picasso sculpture.

MR. KUNSTLER: Who were those seven people?

THE WITNESS: Jerry Rubin. Stew Albert, Wolfe Lowenthal, myself is four; I am not sure of the names of the other three.

MR. KUNSTLER: What were you doing when you were arrested?

THE WITNESS: We were arrested announcing the pig's candidacy for President.

MR. KUNSTLER: Did Jerry Rubin speak?

THE WITNESS: Yes, Jerry Rubin was reading a prepared speech for the pig—the opening sentence was something like, "I, Pigasus, hereby announce my candidacy for the Presidency of the United States." He was interrupted in his talk by the police who arrested us.

MR. KUNSTLER: What was the pig doing during this announcement?

MR. FORAN: Objection.

MR. KUNSTLER: Do you remember what you were charged with?

THE WITNESS: I believe the original charge mentioned was something about an old Chicago law about bringing livestock into the city, or disturbing the peace, or disorderly conduct, and when it came time for the trial, I believe the charge was disorderly conduct.

MR. KUNSTLER: Were you informed by an officer that the pig had squealed on you?

MR. FORAN: Objection. I ask it be stricken.

THE WITNESS: Yes.

THE COURT: I sustain the objection. When an objection is made do not answer until the Court has ruled. . .

\* \* \* \* \* \*

MR. KUNSTLER: Now, I call your attention to Sunday, August 25, 1968. Did you have any occasion to see Jerry Rubin?

---

THE WITNESS: Well, ultimately I saw him at his apartment in Old Town that night.

MR. KUNSTLER: Do you remember approximately what time that was?

THE WITNESS: I guess it was around, maybe, 9:30 approximately 9:30, 10:00. He was laying in bed. He said he was very ill. He was very pale. We had agreed to go to Lincoln Park that night, and so I said, "I hope you are still going to Lincoln Park." He said, "I don't know if I can make it, I seem to he very ill." I cajoled him, and I said, I said, "Come on, you're one of the Yippies. You can't not go to Lincoln Park." He said, "OK," and he got up, and he went to Lincoln Park with me, and I believe Nancy, his girlfriend, and my girlfriend Karen, the four of us walked from his apartment to Lincoln Park.

MR. KUNSTLER: And did you enter the park?

THE WITNESS: Just the outskirts, I mean we basically stood in front of the Lincoln Hotel, and walked across the street from the Lincoln Hotel and stood in the outskirts of the park.

MR. KUNSTLER: Now, did there come a time when people began to leave Lincoln Park?

THE WITNESS: Yes, I guess it was around eleven o'clock at night.

MR. KUNSTLER: What did you do at that time?

THE WITNESS: Continued standing there. We stood there and watched them run right at us, as a matter of fact.

MR. KUNSTLER: Who was with you at this time?

THE WITNESS: The same people I mentioned before.

MR. KUNSTLER: Had you been together continuously since you first left the apartment?

THE WITNESS: Continuously.

MR. KUNSTLER: And from the time you left the apartment to this time, did you see Jerry Rubin wearing a helmet at any time?

THE WITNESS: No.

MR. KUNSTLER: By the way, how long have you known Jerry Rubin?

THE WITNESS: I have known Jerry Rubin approximately four years.

MR. KUNSTLER: Have you ever seen him smoke a cigarette?

THE WITNESS: No.

MR. KUNSTLER: Mr. Ochs, you said there came a time when you left the area. Where did you go?

THE WITNESS: We walked through the streets following the crowd.

MR. KUNSTLER: And can you describe what you saw as you followed the crowd?

THE WITNESS: They were just chaotic and sort of unformed, and people just continued away from the park and just seemed to move, I think toward the commercial area of Old Town where the nightclubs are and then police clubs were there too, and it was just a flurry of movement of people all kinds of ways.

MR. SCHULTZ: If the Court please, the witness was asked what he observed and that was not responsive to the question. If you would simply tell the witness to listen carefully to the question so he can answer the questions.

THE COURT: I did that this morning. You are a singer but you are a smart fellow, I am sure.

THE WITNESS: Thank you very much. You are a judge and you are a smart fellow.

THE COURT: I must ask you to listen carefully to the questions of the lawyer and answer the question. Answer the questions; do not go beyond them.

MR. KUNSTLER: At any time, did you see Jerry Rubin enter Lincoln Park?

THE WITNESS: No.

MR. KUNSTLER: Now, Mr. Ochs, I call your attention to sometime in the vicinity of 6:00 p.m. Tuesday, August 27. Did you see Jerry Rubin?

THE WITNESS: Yes, in Lincoln Park. He asked me to come and sing at a meeting.

MR. KUNSTLER: Do you know what time approximately you sang after arriving there, how long after arriving there?

THE WITNESS: Approximately a half-hour.

MR. KUNSTLER: Was anything happening in that half-hour while you were there?

THE WITNESS: Bobby Seale was speaking.

MR. KUNSTLER: Did Jerry Rubin speak at all?

THE WITNESS: Yes, after I sang.

MR. KUNSTLER: Did you sing a song that day?

THE WITNESS: Yes, "I Ain't Marching Anymore."

MR. KUNSTLER: Did you sing at anybody's request?

THE WITNESS: At Jerry Rubin's request.

MR. KUNSTLER: I am showing you what has been marked at D-147 for identification and I ask you if you can identify that exhibit.

THE WITNESS: This is the guitar I played "I Ain't Marching Anymore" on.

THE COURT: How can you tell? You haven't even looked at it.

THE WITNESS: It is my case.

THE COURT: Are you sure the guitar is in there?

THE WITNESS: I am checking.

MR. KUNSTLER: Open it up, Mr. Ochs, and see whether that is your guitar.

THE WITNESS: That is it, that is it.

MR. KUNSTLER: Now, would you stand and sing that song so the jury can hear the song that the audience heard that day?

MR. SCHULTZ: If the Court please, this is a trial in the Federal District Court. It is not a theater. We don't have to sit and listen to the witness sing a song. Let's get on with the trial. I object.

MR. KUNSTLER: Your Honor, this is definitely an issue in the case. Jerry Rubin has asked for a particular song to be sung. What the witness sang to the audience reflects both on Jerry Rubin's intent and on the mood of the crowd.

THE COURT: I sustain the objection.

MR. KUNSTLER: Your Honor, he is prepared to sing it exactly as he sang it on that day,

THE COURT: I am not prepared to listen, Mr. Kunstler.

MR. KUNSTLER: Do you recall how long after you sang in Lincoln Park that you were somewhere else?

THE WITNESS: I arrived at the next place around seven-thirty, quarter to eight at the Coliseum.

MR. KUNSTLER: Were any of the defendants present at that time?

THE WITNESS: Abbie Hoffman was there, and I do not remember if Jerry Rubin was there.

MR. KUNSTLER: Where did you see Abbie Hoffman first that night at the Coliseum?

THE WITNESS: When he raced in front of me on the stage when I was introduced to Ed Sanders. He said, "Here's Phil Ochs," and as I walked forward, Abbie Hoffman raced in front of me and took the microphone and proceeded to give a speech. I was upstaged by Abbie Hoffman.

MR. KUNSTLER: At the time when you first saw Abbie Hoffman there that night, can you approximate as best you can the time it was when you first saw him take the microphone?

THE WITNESS: Approximately 8:30.

MR. KUNSTLER: Your Honor, I have no further questions.

\* \* \* \* \* \*

MR. SCHULTZ: You were at the Bandshell, were you not?

THE WITNESS: Yes.

MR. SCHULTZ: What time did you arrive at the Bandshell?

THE WITNESS: I don't remember. I'd guess it was around three or after in the afternoon.

MR. FORAN: You seem to have a little trouble with time. Do you carry a watch with you?

THE WITNESS: Just lately.

MR. FORAN: As a matter of fact, when it comes to time during that week, it is pretty much of a guess, isn't it?

THE WITNESS: I guess so.

MR. FORAN: And the time you arrived at the Coliseum it was 9:00 or 9:30, isn't that right? Or at 6:00 or 6:30?

THE WITNESS: No, because the normal opening time of the shows was around 8:00 and I think the show was starting when I got there. That is a safer guess than the other time.

MR. FORAN: It is still a guess though, isn't it?

THE WITNESS: Yes, it is a guess.

MR. SCHULTZ: And now you say at the Coliseum, Abbie Hoffman upstaged you, is that right?

THE WITNESS: Yes. I was walking toward the microphone and he raced in front of me.

MR. SCHULTZ: And he led the crowd in a chant of "Fuck LBJ" didn't he?

THE WITNESS: Yes, yes, I think he did.

MR. SCHULTZ: You didn't remember that on direct examination very well, didn't you?

THE WITNESS: I guess not.

MR. SCHULTZ: Abbie Hoffman is a friend of yours, isn't he?

THE WITNESS: Yes and no.

MR. SCHULTZ: Now in your plans for Chicago, did you plan for public fornication in the park?

THE WITNESS: I didn't.

MR. SCHULTZ: In your discussions with either Rubin or Hoffman did you plan for public fornication in the park?

THE WITNESS: No, we did not seriously sit down and plan public fornication in the park.

MR. SCHULTZ: Did Rubin say at any of these meetings that you must cause disruptions during the Convention and on through Election Day, mass disruptions?

THE WITNESS: No.

MR. SCHULTZ: Was there any discussion when you were planning your Yippie programs by either Rubin or Hoffman of going into the downtown area and taking over hotels for sleeping space?

THE WITNESS: No.

MR. SCHULTZ: Did the defendant Rubin during your planning discussion tell you if he ever had the opportunity and at one of his earliest opportunities he would, when he found some policemen who were isolated in the park, draw a crowd around him and bring the crowd to the policemen and attack the policemen with rocks and stones and bottles, and shout profanities at the policemen, tell them to take off their guns and fight? Did he ever say he was going to do that?

THE WITNESS: No, he didn't, Mr. Schultz.

MR. SCHULTZ: Now, Mr. Ochs, you say that on Sunday night you were with Mr. Rubin all night, is that right?

THE WITNESS: From 9:30 maybe, until after 12:00.

MR. SCHULTZ: And of course you have been told by somebody that there is evidence that Mr. Rubin was in Lincoln Park that night, isn't that right? Well, were you told, or not?

THE WITNESS: Yes.

MR. SCHULTZ: Were you told that somebody saw him with a cigarette in his hand?

THE WITNESS: No, I was not told that.

MR. SCHULTZ: Well, what were you told, please?

THE WITNESS: I was told very little. I was told that Jerry was accused of something

MR. SCHULTZ: Who told you all these things?

THE WITNESS: Mr. Kunstler told me the one thing, not all these things, something that Jerry was accused of something in the park on Sunday night, and that's all I was told, nothing else.

MR. SCHULTZ: You don't want to get Mr. Kunstler into trouble, do you?

MR. KUNSTLER: Your Honor, first of all—

MR. SCHULTZ: Suddenly he backs off—suddenly he backs off. It is all too patent, your Honor.

THE COURT: Will the record show that Mr. Kunstler—

MR. KUNSTLER: Yes, I did, your Honor, I think it is a disgraceful statement in front of a jury.

THE COURT: --threw a block of papers noisily to the floor.

MR. KUNSTLER: All right. I dropped papers noisily to the floor.

THE COURT: I shall not hear from you in that tone, sir.

MR. KUNSTLER: I am sorry for putting the paper on the table, and it fell off onto the floor, but to say in front of a jury, "That is too patent" and "What are you backing off for?" I think, your Honor, any Court in the land would hold that is unconscionable conduct, and if I am angry, I think I am righteously so in this instance.

THE COURT: That will be all.

Continue with your cross-examination.

MR. SCHULTZ: In any event, Mr. Ochs, you are absolutely sure you never really went beyond the fringes of the park with Jerry Rubin that night, isn't that right?

THE WITNESS: Yes.

MR. SCHULTZ: You just stood right along the fringes all that night, you never went in to see what was happening at the command post, did you?

THE WITNESS: No.

MR. SCHULTZ: You never walked in to see what was happening at the fieldhouse, did you?

THE WITNESS: No.

MR. SCHULTZ: That is all, your Honor.

THE COURT: You may step down.

   (*witness excused*)


THE COURT: Don't forget your guitar.

THE WITNESS: I won't.

THE COURT: Call your next witness.

# Testimony Of Allen Ginsberg

MR. WEINGLASS: Will you please state your full name?

THE WITNESS: Allen Ginsberg.

MR. WEINGLASS: What is your Occupation?

THE WITNESS: Poet.

MR. WEINGLASS: Have you authored any books in the field of poetry?

THE WITNESS: In 1956, *Howl and other Poems*; in 1960, *Kaddish and other poems*; in 1963, *Empty Mirror*; in 1963, *Reality Sandwiches*, and in 1969, *Planet News*.

MR. WEINGLASS: Now, in addition to your writing, Mr. Ginsberg, are you presently engaged in any other activity?

THE WITNESS: I teach, lecture, and recite poetry at universities.

MR. WEINGLASS: Now, did you ever study abroad?

THE WITNESS: Yes. In India and Japan.

MR. WEINGLASS: Could you indicate for the court and jury what the area of your studies consisted of?

THE WITNESS: Mantra Yoga, meditation exercises and sitting quietly, breathing exercises to calm the body and calm the mind, but mainly a branch called Mantra Yoga, which is yoga which involved prayer and chanting.

MR. WEINGLASS: How long did you study?

THE WITNESS: I was in India for a year and a third, and then in Japan studying with Gary Snyder, a zen poet, at Dai Tokuji Monastery, D-A-I T-O-K-U-J-I. I sat there for the zazen exercises for centering the body and quieting the mind.

MR. WEINGLASS: Are you still studying under any of your former teachers?

THE WITNESS: Yes, Swami Bahkti Vedanti, faith, philosophy; Bahkti Vedanta, B-A-H-K-T-I V-E-D-A-N-T-A. I have seen him and chanted within the last few years in different cities, and he has asked me to continue chanting, especially on public occasions. This involves chanting and praying, praying out loud and in community.

MR. WEINGLASS: In the course of a Mantra chant, is there any particular position that the person doing that assumes?

THE WITNESS: Any position which will let the stomach relax and be easy, fall out, so that aspiration can be deep into the body, to relax the body completely and calm the mind, based as cross-legged.

MR. WEINGLASS: And is it—chanting—to be done privately, or is it in public?

MR. FORAN: Oh, your Honor, I object. I think we have gone far enough now—

THE COURT: I think I have a vague idea now of the witness' profession. It is vague.

MR. FORAN: I think I might also indicate that he is an excellent speller.

THE WITNESS: Sir—

THE COURT: Yes, sir.

THE WITNESS: In India, the profession of poetry and the profession of chanting are linked together as one practice.

THE COURT: That's right, I give you credit for that.

MR. WEINGLASS: Mr. Ginsberg, do you know the defendant Jerry Rubin?

THE WITNESS: Yes, I do.

MR. WEINGLASS: Do you recall where it was that you first met him?

THE WITNESS: In Berkeley and San Francisco in 1965 during the time of the anti-Vietnam war marches in Berkeley. I saw him again at the human be-in in San Francisco. We shared the stage with many other people.

MR. WEINGLASS: Would you describe for the Court and jury what the be-in in San Francisco was?

THE WITNESS: A large assembly of younger people who came together to—

MR. FORAN: Objection, your Honor.

THE COURT: Just a minute, I am not sure how you spell the be-in.

MR. WEINGLASS: B-E I-N, I believe, be-in.

THE WITNESS: Human be-in.

THE COURT: I really can't pass on the validity of the objection because I don't understand the question.

MR. WEINGLASS: I asked him to explain what a be-in was.

MR. FORAN: I would love to know also but I don't think it has anything to do with this lawsuit.

THE COURT: I will over the objection of the Government, tell what a be-in is.

THE WITNESS: A gathering-together of younger people aware of the planetary fate that we are all sitting in the middle of, imbued with a new consciousness, a new kind of society involving prayer, music, and spiritual life together rather than competition, acquisition and war.

MR. WEINGLASS: And was that the activity that was engaged in in San Francisco at this be-in?

WITNESS: There was what was called a "gathering of the tribes" of all the different affinity groups, spiritual groups, political group, yoga groups, music groups and poetry groups that all felt the same crisis of identity crisis of the planet and political crisis in America, who all came together in the largest assemblage of such younger people that had taken place since the war in the presence of the Zen master Sazuki and in the presence of the rock bands and the presence of Timothy Leary and Mr. Rubin.

MR. WEINGLASS: Now, later on in the year of 1967 did you have occasion to meet again with the defendant Jerry Rubin?

THE WITNESS: Yes, we met in a cafe in Berkeley and discussed his mayoral race for the city of Berkeley. He had run for mayor.

MR. WEINGLASS: Did you have any participation in that campaign?

THE WITNESS: I encouraged it, blessed it.

MR. WEINGLASS: Now, do you know the defendant Abbie Hoffman?

THE WITNESS: Yes.

MR. WEINGLASS: Now, calling your attention to the month of February 1968, did you have any occasion in that month to meet with Abbie Hoffman?

THE WITNESS: Yeah.

MR. WEINGLASS: Do you recall what Mr. Hoffman said in the course of the conversation.

THE WITNESS: Yippee—among other things. He said that politics had become theater and magic; that it was the manipulation of imagery through mass media that was confusing and hypnotizing the people in the United States and making them accept a war which they did not really believe in; that people were involved in a life style that was intolerable to young folks, which involved brutality and police violence as well as a larger violence in Vietnam; and that ourselves might be able to get together in Chicago and invite teachers to present different ideas of what is wrong with the planet, what we can do to solve the pollution crisis, what we can do to solve the Vietnam war, to present different ideas for making the society more sacred and less commercial, less materialistic; what we could do to uplevel or improve the whole tone of the trap that we all felt ourselves in as the population grew and as politics became more and more violent and chaotic.

MR. WEINGLASS: Now, did he ascribe any particular name to that project?

THE WITNESS: Festival of life.

MR. WEINGLASS: After he spoke to you, what, if anything, was your response to suggestion?

THE WITNESS: I was worried whether or not the whole scene would get violent. I was worried whether we would be allowed to put on such a situation allowed to put. I was worried, you know, whether the government would let us do something that was funnier or prettier or more charming than what was going to be going on in the Convention hall.

MR. FORAN: I object and ask that it be stricken. It was not responsive.

THE COURT: Yes. I sustain the objection.

THE WITNESS: Sir, that was our conversation.

MR, WEINGLASS: Now, during that same month, February of 1968, did you have occasion to meet with Jerry Rubin?

THE WITNESS: I spoke with Jerry Rubin on the phone, I believe.

MR. WEINGLASS: Will you relate to the Court and jury what Jerry Rubin said to you?

THE WITNESS: Jerry told me that he and others were going to Chicago to apply for permission from the city government for a permit to hold a Festival of Life and that he was talking with John Sinclair about getting rock and roll bands together and other musicians and that he would report back to me.

MR. WEINGLASS: Mr. Ginsberg, do you recall anything else that Mr. Rubin said to you in the course of that telephone conversation?

THE WITNESS: Yes, he said that he thought it would be interesting if we could get up little schools like ecology schools, music schools, political schools, schools about the Vietnam war, schools with yogis. He asked if I could contact Burroughs and ask Burroughs to come to teach nonverbal, nonconceptual feeling states.

MR. WEINGLASS: Now you indicated a school of ecology. Could you explain to the Court and jury what that is?

THE WITNESS: Ecology is the interrelation of all the living forms on the surface of the planet involving the food chain—that is to say, whales eat plankton: larger fishes eat smaller fish, octopus or squid eat shellfish which eat plankton; human beings eat the shellfish or squid or smaller fish which eat the smaller tiny microorganisms

MR. FORAN: That is enough, your Honor.

THE COURT: Yes. We all have a clear idea of what ecology is.

THE WITNESS: Well, the destruction of ecology is what would have been taught. That is, how it is being destroyed by human intervention and messing it up with pollution.

MR. WEINGLASS: Now you also indicated that Mr. Rubin mentioned nonverbal education. Will you explain what that is to the Court and jury?

THE WITNESS: Most of our consciousness, since we are continually looking at images on television and listening to words, reading newspapers, talking in courts such as this, most of our consciousness is filled with language, with a kind of matter babble behind the ear, a continuous yakety-yak that actually prevents us from breathing deeply in our bodies and sensing more subtly and sweetly the feelings that we actually do have as persons to each other rather than as talking machines.

MR. WEINGLASS: Now, Mr. Ginsberg, on March 17, where were you?

THE WITNESS: I took part in a press conference fit the Hotel Americana in New York City.

MR. WEINGLASS: Who else was present at this press conference?

THE WITNESS: Abbie Hoffman and Jerry Rubin were there as well as Phil Ochs, the folk singer, Arlo Guthrie, some members of the USA band, some members of the Diggers groups.

MR. WEINGLASS: Could you indicate to the Court and jury what Jerry Rubin said?

THE WITNESS: He said that a lot of younger people in America would come to Chicago during the Convention and hold a Festival of Life in the parks, and he announced that they were negotiating with the City Hall to get a permit to have a life festival in the parks.

MR. WEINGLASS: Do you recall what Abbie Hoffman said?

THE WITNESS: He said that they were going to go to Chicago in groups to negotiate with representatives of Mayor Daley to get a permit for a large-scale Gathering of the Tribes and he mentioned the human be-in in San Francisco.

MR. WEINGLASS: Did you yourself participate in that press conference?

THE WITNESS: Yes. I stepped to the microphone also. My statement was that the planet Earth at the present moment was endangered by violence, overpopulation, pollution, ecological destruction brought about by our own greed; that our younger children in America and other countries of the world might not survive the next thirty years; that it was a planetary crisis that had not been recognized by any government of the world and had not been recognized by our own government, nor the politicians who were preparing for the elections; that the younger people of America were aware of that and that precisely was what was called psychedelic consciousness; that we were going to gather together as we had before in the San Francisco human be-in to manifest our presence over and above the presence of the more selfish elder politicians who were not thinking in terms of what their children would need in future generations, or even in the generation immediately coming, or even for themselves in their own lifetime and were continuing to threaten the planet with violence, with war, with mass murder, with germ warfare. And since the younger people knew that in the United States, we are going to invite them there, find that the central motive would be a presentation of a desire for the preservation of the planet. The desire for preservation of the planet and the planet's form was manifested to my mind by the great Mantra from India to the preserver god Vishnu whose Mantra is the Hare Krishna. And then I chanted the Hare Krishna for ten minutes to the television cameras, and it goes:

Hare krishna/hare krishna/krishna krishna/hare hare/hare rama/hare rama/rama rama/hare hare.

MR. WEINGLASS: Now in chanting that did you have all accompaniment of any particular instrument? Your Honor, I object to the laughter of the Court on this. I think this is a serious presentation of a religious concept.

THE COURT: I don't understand. I don't understand it because it was—the language of the United States District Court is English.

MR. KUNSTLER: I know, but you don't laugh at all languages.

THE COURT: I didn't laugh. I didn't laugh.

THE WITNESS: I would be happy to explain it.

THE COURT: I didn't laugh at all. I wish I could tell you how I feel. Laugh—I didn't even smile.

MR. KUNSTLER: Well, I thought—

THE COURT: All I could tell you is that I didn't understand it because whatever language the witness is using—

THE WITNESS: Sanskrit, sir.

THE COURT: Well, that is one I don't know. That is the reason I didn't understand it.

THE WITNESS: Might we go on to an explanation?

THE COURT: Will you keep quiet, Mr. Witness, while I am talking to the lawyers?

THE WITNESS: I will be glad to give an explanation.

THE COURT: I never laugh at a witness, sir. I protect witnesses who come to this court. But I do tell you that the language of the American court is English unless you have an interpreter. You may use an interpreter for the remainder of the witness' testimony.

MR. KUNSTLER: No. I have heard, Your Honor, priests explain the mass in Latin in American courts and I think Mr. Ginsberg is doing exactly the same thing in Sanskrit for another type of religious experience.

THE COURT: I don't understand Sanskrit. I venture to say the jury members don't. Perhaps we have some people on the jury who do understand Sanskrit, I don't know, but I wouldn't even have known it was Sanskrit until he told me. I can't see that that is material to the issues here, that is all.

MR. WEINGLASS: Let me ask this: Mr. Ginsberg, I show you an object marked 150 for identification, and I ask you to examine that object.

THE WITNESS: Yes.

MR. FORAN: All right. Your Honor, that is enough. I object to it, your Honor. I think it is outrageous for counsel to —

THE COURT: You asked him to examine it, fine, instead of that he played a tune on it. I sustain the objection.

THE WITNESS: It adds spirituality to the case, sir.

THE COURT: Will you remain quiet, sir.

'THE WITNESS: I am sorry.

MR. WEINGLASS: Having examined that, could you identify it for the court and jury?

THE WITNESS: It is an instrument known as the harmonium, which I used at the press conference at the Americana Hotel. It is commonly used in India.

MR. FORAN: I object to that.

THE COURT: I sustain the objection.

MR. WEINGLASS: Will you explain to the Court and to the jury what chant you were chanting at the press conference?

THE WITNESS: I was chanting a mantra called the "Mala Mantra," the great mantra of preservation of that aspect of the Indian religion called Vishnu the Preserver. Every time human evil rises so high that the planet itself is threatened, and all of its inhabitants and their children are threatened, Vishnu will preserve a return.

MR. WEINGLASS: Directing your attention to the month of April 1965, did you have occasion during that month to meet with the defendant Jerry Rubin?

THE WITNESS: Yes.

MR. WEINGLASS: What, if anything, did Jerry Rubin say?

THE WITNESS: He said that to insure a peaceful gathering in Chicago, so that a lot of people would come, encouraged by the peaceful nature of it, that they were applying as a group to the Chicago mayor's office to get a permit, but that apparently they were having trouble getting the permit. They would continue negotiating with the City, with City Hall for that permit. He said he felt that the only way a lot of people would come is if there were really good vibrations coming out of us and that he wanted it to be a peaceful gathering. I told him I was scared of getting into a scene where I would get beaten up or a mob scene because I was not used to that and I didn't want to, I was just simply frightened of too large a gathering which would involve conflict and fighting and getting my head busted in, and so I asked him how he felt about it, whether he was going to work for an actually peaceful gathering or not, because I didn't want to participate unless it was going to be organized peacefully, and he said he wanted it to be peaceful because he wanted a lot of people there.

MR. WEINGLASS: Now, directing your attention to August 13 at approximately 5:30 in the afternoon, where were you in the city of Chicago?

THE WITNESS: I went up to City Hall to the mayor's office. I told Mr. Stahl that I was afraid of getting into a violent scene. I chanted the Hare Krishna mantra to Mr. Stahl and Mr. Bush as an example of what was intended by the Festival of Life and I asked them to please give a permit to avoid violence.

MR. WEINGLASS: Could you chant for the Court and the jury the mantra Hare Krishna as you did that day?

MR. FORAN: Objection.

THE COURT: I sustain the objection.

MR. WEINGLASS: Could you speak without chanting for the Court and jury the Mantra Hare Krishna?

THE WITNESS: Hare krishna/hare krishna

MR. FORAN: I object.

THE COURT: I sustain the objection.

MR. WEINGLASS: Directing your attention to the morning of August 24, 1968, where were you?

THE WITNESS: I was on a plane coming from New York to Chicago.

MR. WEINGLASS: Now, en route to Chicago while you were on the plane, what if anything, did you do?

THE WITNESS: I wrote poetry, wrote out a statement of what I thought was going on in Chicago at the time.

MR. WEINGLASS: Could you read to the jury that poem?

THE WITNESS: Gladly. I believe you have the text. August 24, 1968/Going to Chicago 22,000 feet over hazed square vegetable plant floor/Approaching Chicago to die or flying over earth another 40 years to die/Indifferent and afraid, that the bone shattering bullet be the same/As the vast evaporation of phenomena cancer come true in an old man's bed/Or the historic fire heaven descending 22,000 years end the Aeon./The lake's blue again, sky's the same baby, though papers and noses rumor star/Spread the natural universe'll make angels' feet sticky./I heard the Angel King's voice a bodiless timeful teenager/Eternal in my own heart, saying Trust the purest joy,/Democratic anger is an illusion, democratic Joy is God,/Our father is baby blue, the original face you see, sees you./How through conventional notice and revolutionary fury remember/The helpless order the police armed to protect the helpless freedom to protect, the helpless freedom the revolutionary/Conspired to honor? I am the Angel King saying the Angel King/As the mobs in the Ampitheatre, streets, Coliseums, parks and offices/Scream in despair over meat and metal Microphone.

MR. WEINGLASS: At approximately 10:30, August 24, where were you?

THE WITNESS: I was in Lincoln Park.

MR. WEINGLASS: And what occurred in Lincoln Park approximately 10:30, if you can recall?

THE WITNESS: There were several thousand young people gathered, waiting, late at night. It was dark. There were some bonfires burning in trashcans. Everybody was standing around not knowing what to do. Suddenly there was a great deal of consternation and movement and shouting among the crowd in the park, and I turned, surprised, because it was early. The police were or had given 11:00 as the date or as the time—

MR. FORAN: Objection, your Honor.

MR. WEINGLASS: What did you do at the time you saw the police do this?

THE WITNESS: I started the chant, O-o-m-m-m-m-m-, O-o-m-m-m-m-m-m.

M R. FORAN: All right, we have had a demonstration.

THE COURT: All right.

MR. WEINGLASS : Did you finish your answer?

THE WITNESS: We walked out of the park. We continued chanting for at least twenty minutes, slowly gathering other people, chanting, Ed Sanders and I in the center, until there were a group of maybe fifteen or twenty making a very solid heavy vibrational change of aim that penetrated the immediate area around us, and attracted other people, and so we walked out slowly toward the street, toward Lincoln Park.

MR. WEINGLASS: I now show you what is marked D-153 for identification. Could you read that to the jury?

THE WITNESS: Magic Password Bulletin. Physic Jujitsu. In case of hysteria, the magic password is o-m, same as o-h-m-, which cuts through all emergency illusions. Pronounce o-m from the middle of the body, diaphragm or solar plexus. Ten people humming o-m can calm down one himself. One hundred people humming o-m can regulate the metabolism of a thousand. A thousand bodies vibrating o-m can immobilize an entire downtown Chicago street full of scared humans, uniformed or naked. Signed, Allen Ginsberg, Ed Sanders. O-m will be practiced on the beach at sunrise ceremonies with Allen and Ed.

MR. WEINGLASS: Could you explain to the Court and jury what you meant in that last statement of your message?

THE WITNESS: By "immobilize" I meant shut down the mental machinery which repeats over and over again the images of fear which are scaring people in uniform, that is to say, the police officers or the demonstrators, who I refer to as naked meaning naked emotionally, and perhaps hopefully naked physically.

MR. WEINGLASS: And what did you intend to create by having that mechanism shut down?

THE WITNESS: A completely peaceful realization of the fact that we were all stuck in the same street, place, terrified of each other, and reacting in panic and hysteria rather than reacting with awareness of each other as human beings, as people with bodies that actually feel, can chant and pray and have a certain sense of vibration to each other or tenderness to each other which is basically what everybody wants, rather than fear.

MR. WEINGLASS: Now directing your attention to the next day which is Sunday, August 25, what, if anything, did you do in the park?

THE WITNESS: First I walked around to the center of the park, where suddenly a group of policemen appeared in the middle of the younger people. There was an appearance of a great mass of policemen going through the center of the park. I was afraid then, thinking they were going to make trouble—

MR. FORAN: Objection to his state of mind.

THE COURT: I sustain the objection.

MR. WEINGLASS: What did you do when you saw the policemen in the center of the crowd?

THE WITNESS: Adrenalin ran through my body. I sat down on a green hillside with a group of younger people that were walking with me about 3:30 in the afternoon, 4:00 o'clock. Sat, crossed my legs, and began chanting O-o-m, O-o-m-m-m-m, O-o-m-m-m-m, O-o-m-m-m-m.

MR. FORAN: I gave him four that time.

THE WITNESS: I continued chanting for several hours.

THE COURT: Did you say you continued chanting seven hours?

THE WITNESS: Seven hours, yes. About six hours I chanted "Om" and for the seventh hour concluded with the chant Hare krishna/hare krishna/krishna krishna/hare hare/ hare rima/hare rama/rama rama/hare hare.

MR. WEINGLASS: Now, directing your attention to Monday night, that is August 26, in the evening, where were you?

THE WITNESS: I was by a barricade that was set up, a pile of trash cans and police barricades, wooden horses, I believe. There were a lot of young kids, some black, some white, shouting and beating on the tin barrels, making a fearsome noise.

MR. WEINGLASS: What did you do after you got there?

THE WITNESS: Started chanting "Om." For a while I was joined in the chant by a lot of young people who were there until the chant encompassed most of the people by the barricade, and we raised a huge loud sustained series of "Oms" into the air loud enough to include everybody. Just as it reached, like, a great unison crescendo, all of a sudden a police car came rolling down into the group, right into the center of the group where I was standing, and with a lot of crashing and tinkling sound of glass, and broke up the chanting, broke up the unison and the physical—everybody was holding onto each other physically—broke up that physical community that had been built and broke up the sound chant that had been built. I moved back. There was a crash of glass.

MR. WEINGLASS: What occurred at that time?

THE WITNESS: I started moving away from the scene. I started moving away from the scene because there was violence there.

MR. WEINGLASS: Mr. Ginsberg, very early in the morning, about 6:00 A.M. on Tuesday, where were you?

THE WITNESS: I was on the bench at the lakefront at Lincoln Park, conducting a mantra chant ceremony, that had been arranged to be performed by Abbie Hoffman and Jerry Rubin, and the other people who were planning the weekly schedule of Yippie activities.

MR. WEINGLASS: What occurred at this ritual?

THE WITNESS: We got together to greet the morning with Tibetan Buddhist magic prayer formulas, mantras, beginning with Om raksa/raksa hum/hum/phat/svaha, the mantra to purify a site for the ceremony.

MR. WEINGLASS: Now, at approximately 8:00 p.m. where were you?

THE WITNESS: I came with a party of writers to the unbirthday party of President Johnson at the Coliseum.

MR. WEINGLASS: Who was with you?

THE WITNESS: The French writer, Jean Genet, poet novelist. The American novelist, William Seward. W. S. Burroughs, the novelist. The novelist, Terry Southern, who had written Doctor Strangelove. Myself. We all write together.

MR. WEINGLASS: Now, when you arrived at the Coliseum, did you see any of the defendants present?

THE WITNESS: Abbie Hoffman. I went down and sat next to him and kissed him, and then pointed back up at Jean Genet and told Abbie that Genet was there.

MR. WEINGLASS: Where, if anywhere, did you go?

THE WITNESS: The group I was with, Mr. Genet, Mr. Burroughs, and Mr. Seaver, and Terry Southern, all went back to Lincoln Park.

MR. WEINGLASS: What was occurring at the park as you got there?

THE WITNESS: There was a great crowd lining the outskirts of the park and a little way into the park on the inner roads, and there was a larger crowd moving in toward the center. We all moved in toward the center, and at the center of the park, there was a group of ministers and rabbis who had elevated a great cross about ten-foot high in the middle of a circle of people who were sitting around, quietly, listening to the ministers conduct a ceremony.

MR. WEINGLASS: And would you relate to the Court and jury what was being said and done at the time?

THE WITNESS: Everybody was seated around the cross, which was at the center of hundreds of people, people right around the very center adjoining the cross. Everybody was singing, "We Shall Overcome," and "Onward Christian Soldiers," I believe. They were old hymn times. I was seated with my friends on a little hillock looking down on the crowd, which had the cross in the center. And on the other side, there were a lot of glary lights hundreds of feet away down the field. The ministers lifted up the cross and took it to the edge of the crowd and set it down facing the lights where the police were. In other words, they confronted the police lines with the cross of Christ.

MR. WEINGLASS: And after the ministers moved the cross, what happened?

THE WITNESS: After, I don't know, a short period of time, there was a burst of smoke and tear gas around the cross, and the cross was enveloped with tear gas, and the people who were carrying the cross were enveloped with tear gas which began slowly drifting over the crowd.

MR. WEINGLASS: And when you saw the persons with the cross and the cross being gassed, what, if anything, did you do?

THE WITNESS: I turned to Burroughs and said, "They have gassed the cross of Christ."

MR. FORAN: Objection, if the Court please.

MR. WEINGLASS: What did you do at that time?

THE WITNESS: I took Bill Burroughs' hand, and took Terry Southern's hand, and we turned from the cross which was covered with gas in the glary lights, the police lights that were shining through the tear gas on the cross, and walked slowly out of the park.

MR. WEINGLASS: On Wednesday, the next day, at approximately 3:45 in the afternoon, do you recall where you were?

THE WITNESS: Yes. Entering the Grant Park Bandshell area, where there was a mobilization meeting or rally going on. I was still with the same group of literary fellows, poets and writers. I walked tip to the apron or front of the stage, and saw David Dellinger and told him that I was there, and that Burroughs was there and Jean Genet was there and that they were all willing to be present and testify to the righteousness of the occasion, and that we would like to be on the stage.

MR. WEINGLASS: Were you then introduced?

THE WITNESS: Yes. Jean Genet was also introduced.

MR. WEINGLASS: Did you speak?

THE WITNESS: I croaked, yes.

THE COURT: What was that last? You say you what?

THE WITNESS: I croaked. My voice was gone. I chanted or tried to chant.

MR. WEINGLASS: Did you remain for the rest of the rally?

THE WITNESS: Yes. I didn't pay much attention to most of the speakers that followed. There was one that I heard. Louis Abolafia, whom I knew from New York.

MR. WEINGLASS: And who is he?

THE WITNESS: Kind of a Bohemian trickster, street theater candidate for President. He had announced his candidacy for President a number of times, and his campaign slogan was, "I have nothing to hide," and he showed himself in a photograph with his hand over his lap, but otherwise naked.

MR. WEINGLASS: Was he introduced?

THE WITNESS: No, he just appeared from nowhere and got up to the microphone and started yelling into it.

MR. WEINGLASS: Do you recall hearing what he was yelling?

THE WITNESS: "The police out there are armed and violent. You are walking into a death trap."

MR. WEINGLASS: When you heard him yelling that over the microphone, what, if anything, did you do?

THE WITNESS: I went over and sat next to him, and grabbed his leg, and started tickling him, and said, "Hare krishna, Louis."

MR. WEINGLASS: Now, when the rally was over, did you have occasion to talk with Mr. Dellinger?

THE WITNESS: Yes. He looked me in the eyes, took my arm and said, "Allen, will you please march in the front line with me?

MR. WEINGLASS: And what did you say to him?

THE WITNESS: I said, "Well, I am here with Burroughs and Genet and Terry Southern." And he said, "Well, all of you together, can you form a front line and be sure to stay behind me in the front line, be the first of the group of marchers?"

MR. WEINGLASS: And did you form such a line?

THE WITNESS: Yes.

MR. WEINGLASS: How were you walking?

THE WITNESS: Our arms were all linked together and we were carrying flowers. Someone had brought flowers up to the back of the stage, and so we distributed them around to the front rows of marchers so all the marchers had flowers.

MR. WEINGLASS: Mr. Ginsberg, I show you a photograph marked D-158 for identification, and I ask you if you can identify that photograph.

THE WITNESS: Yes. It is a picture of the front line of marchers as I described it before, consisting of William Burroughs on the extreme right, Jean Genet, Richard Seaver, his editor at Grove, myself.

MR. WEINGLASS: Now, Mr. Ginsberg, you have indicated you have known Jerry Rubin since 1965?

THE WITNESS: Yes.

MR. WEINGLASS: Would you indicate to the Court and jury whether or not you have ever seen him smoke a cigarette?

THE WITNESS: I don't remember.

MR. WEINGLASS: I mean a tobacco cigarette.

THE WITNESS: Offhand, no.

MR. WEINGLASS: Now, Mr. Ginsberg, you have had extensive training in Zen and in other religions of the East. Have you acquired an expertise in the area of peaceful assembly and peaceful intent?

MR. FORAN: I object to that, Your Honor.

THE COURT: I sustain the objection.

MR. WEINGLASS: Did you see during Convention week either the defendant Jerry Rubin or the defendant Abbie Hoffman or any of the other defendants who are seated at this table commit an act or make a speech or do anything, do any other thing to violate the precepts of your own philosophy?

MR. FORAN: Objection.

THE COURT: I sustain the objection.

MR. WEINGLASS: I have no further questions.

MR. FORAN: Your Honor, I have to get some materials to properly carry on my cross-examination of this witness. It will take some time to go downstairs to get them.

THE COURT: Are you suggesting we recess?

MR. FORAN: I would think yes, your, Honor.

THE COURT: All right. We will go until two o'clock.

MR. KUNSTLER: Your Honor, we asked for five minutes two days ago in front of this jury and you refused to give it to us.

THE COURT: You will have to cease that disrespectful tone.

MR. KUNSTLER: That is not disrespect, that is an angry tone, your Honor.

THE COURT: Yes, it is. Yes, it is. I will grant the motion of the Government.

MR. KUNSTLER: You refused us five minutes the other day.

THE COURT: You are shouting at the Court.

MR. KUNSTLER: Oh, your Honor—

THE COURT: I never shouted at you during this trial.

MR. KUNSTLER: Your Honor, your voice has been raised.

THE COURT: You have been disrespectful.

MR. KUNSTLER: It is not disrespectful, your Honor.

THE COURT: And sometimes worse than that.

THE WITNESS: O-o-m-m-m-m-m-m-m.

THE COURT: Will you step off the witness stand?

MR. KUNSTLER: He was trying to calm us both down, your Honor.

THE COURT: Oh, no. I needed no calming down. That will be all....

THE COURT You have finished your direct? You may cross-examine.

MR. FORAN: Mr. Ginsberg, you were named as kind of the Yippie religious leader. Do you think that is a fair designation of your connection with the Yippie organization?

THE WITNESS: No, because the word "leader" was one we really tried to get away from, to get away from that authoritarian thing. It was more like—

MR. FORAN: Religious teacher?

THE WITNESS: —religious experimenter, or someone who was interested in experimenting with that, and with moving things in that direction.

MR. FORAN: In the context of the Yippie organization?

THE WITNESS: Yes, and also in the context of our whole political life too.

MR. FORAN: And among the others named are Timothy Leary.

THE WITNESS: Yes

MR. FORAN: And Timothy Leary has a kind of religious concept that he attempts to articulate, doesn't he?

THE WITNESS: Yes, it is a religious concept that has a very ancient tradition in Shivite worship and in American Indian worship services or ceremonies.

MR. FORAN: And one of the parts of that religious concept is the religious experience in the use of hallucinogenic drugs, isn't it, Mr. Ginsberg?

THE WITNESS: In India, in the Shivite sect, they refer to it as gunga or bhang, which in Latin is cannabis and which in the American language is marijuana, or pot, or grass.

MR. FORAN: In the course of his teaching, he makes use of those drugs himself?

THE WITNESS: I think he says that they are part of the legitimate religious meditation and worship exercises.

MR. FORAN: Now when you went out to the Coliseum and you met Abbie Hoffman, you said when you met him you kissed him?

THE WITNESS: Yes.

MR FORAN: Is he an intimate friend of yours?

THE WITNESS: I felt very intimate with him. I saw he was struggling to manifest a beautiful thing, and I felt very good towards him.

MR. FORAN: And do you consider him an intimate friend of yours?

THE WITNESS: I don't see him that often, but I do see him often enough and have worked with him often enough to feel intimate with him, yes.

MR. FORAN: You feel pretty much an intimate friend of Jerry Rubin's too?

THE WITNESS: Over the years, I have learned from them both.

MR. FORAN: By the way, you were asked on direct examination whether you had seen Jerry Rubin smoke any tobacco.

THE WITNESS: Yes, I said I didn't remember seeing him smoke.

MR. FORAN: Have you seen him smoke anything?

THE WITNESS: No, I don't remember seeing him smoke anything. I don't remember ever seeing him smoke.

MR. FORAN: Anything?

THE WITNESS: Yes.

MR. FORAN: Now, you testified concerning a number of books of poetry that you have written?

THE WITNESS: Yes.

MR. FORAN: In *The Empty Mirror*, there is a poem called "The Night Apple"?

THE WITNESS: Yes.

MR. FORAN: Would you recite that for the jury?

THE WITNESS: The Night Apple. Last night I dreamed/of one I loved/for seven long years,/but I saw no face,/only the familiar/presence of the body;/sweat skin eyes/feces urine sperm/saliva all one/odor and mortal taste.

MR. FORAN: Could you explain to the jury what the religious significance of that poem is?

THE WITNESS: If you would take a wet dream as a religious experience, I could.  It is a description of a wet dream, sir.

MR. FORAN: Now, I call your attention in that same Government's Exhibit No. 59, to page 14. That has on it the poem, "In Society." Can you recite that poem to the jury?

WITNESS: Yes, I will read it. In Society. I walked into the cocktail party/room and found three or four queers/talking together in queer-talk,/I tried to be friendly but heard/myself talking to one in hiptalk./"I'm glad to see you," he said, and/looked away, "Hmn," I mused.  The room/was small and had a double-decker/bed in it, and cooking apparatus:/icebox, cabinet, toasters, stove;/the hosts seemed to live with room/enough only for cooking and sleeping./My remark on this score was under-/stood but not appreciated, I was/offered refreshments, which I accepted./ I ate a sandwich of pure meat; an/enormous sandwich of human flesh,/l noticed, while I was chewing on it,/it also included a dirty asshole. More company came, including a/fluffy female who looked like/a princess. She glared at me and/said immediately: "I don't like you,"Turned her head away, and refused/to be introduced.  I said "What!"/in outrage. "Why you shit-faced fool!"/This got everybody's attention./"Why you narcissistic bitch! How/can you decide when you don't even/know me," I continued in a violent/and messianic voice, inspired at/last, dominating the whole room. Dream 1947.

It is a record, a literal record of a dream, as the other was a literal record of a dream.

MR. FORAN: Can you explain the religious significance of that poetry?

THE WITNESS: Actually, yes.

MR. FORAN: Would you explain it to the jury?

THE WITNESS: Yes. One of the major yogas, or "yoking" — yoga means yoke — is bringing together the conscious mind with the unconscious mind, and is an examination of dream-states in an attempt to recollect dream-states, no matter how difficult they are, no matter how repulsive they are, even if they include hysteria, sandwiches of human flesh, which include dirty assholes, because those are universal images that come in everybody's dreams, The attempt in yoga is to enlarge consciousness, to be conscious that one's own consciousness will include everything which occurs within the body and the mind. As part of the practice of poetry, I have always kept records of dreams whenever I have remembered them, and have tried not to censor them so that I would have all the evidence to examine in light of day, so that I would find out who I was unconsciously. Part of the Zen meditation and part of yoga meditation consists in the objective impersonal examination of the rise and fall and disappearance of thoughts in the mind, all thoughts, whether they be thoughts of sleeping with one's mother, which is universal, or sleeping with one's father, which is also universal thought, or becoming an angel, or flying, or attending a cocktail party and being afraid of being put down, and then getting hysterical. In other words, the attempt is to reclaim the unconscious, to write down in the light of day what is going on in the deepest meditation of night and dream-state. So it is part of yoga which involves bridging the difference between public, as in this Courtroom, and private subjective public, which is conscious, which we can say to each other in family situations, and private, which is what we know and tell only our deepest friends.

MR. FORAN: Thank you. You also wrote a book of poems called *Reality Sandwiches*, didn't you?

THE WITNESS: Yes.

MR. FORAN: In there, there is a poem called, "Love Poem on Theme by Whitman." Would you recite that to the jury?

THE WITNESS: "Love Poem on Theme by Whitman," Walt Whitman being one celebrated bard, national prophet. The poem begins with a quotation of a line by Walt Whitman. It begins with Walt Whitman's line: I'll go into the bedroom silently and lie down between the bridegroom and the bride,/those bodies fallen from heaven stretched out waiting naked and restless,/arms resting over their eyes in the darkness,/bury my face in their shoulders and breasts, breathing their skin,/and stroke and kiss neck and mouth and make back be open and known,/legs raised up, crook'd to receive, cock in the darkness driven tormented and attacking/roused up from hole to itching head,/bodies locked shuddering naked, hot lips and buttocks screwed into each other/and eyes, eyes glinting and charming, widening into looks and abandon,/and moans of movement, voices, hands in air, hands between thighs,/hands in moisture on softened lips, throbbing contraction of bellies/till the white come flow in the swirling sheets/and the bride cry for forgiveness, and the groom be covered with tears of passion and compassion,/and I rise up from the bed replenished with last intimate gestures and kisses of farewell—/all before the mind wakes, behind shades and closed doors in a darkened house/where the inhabitants roam unsatisfied in the night,/nude ghosts seeking each other out in the silence.

MR. FORAN: Would you explain the religious significance of that poem?

THE WITNESS: As part of our nature, as part of our human nature, we have many loves, many of which are denied, many of which we deny to ourselves. He said that the reclaiming of those loves and the becoming aware of those loves was the only way that this nation could save itself and become a democratic and spiritual republic. He said that unless there were an infusion of feeling, of tenderness, of fearlessness, of spirituality, of natural sexuality, of natural delight in each other's bodies into the hardened, materialistic, cynical, life denying, clearly competitive, afraid, scared, armored bodies, there would be no chance for a spiritual democracy to take place in America. And he defined that tenderness between the citizens as, in his words, an adhesiveness, a natural tenderness flowing between all citizens as, in his words, an adhesiveness, a natural tenderness flowing between all citizens, not only men and women but also a tenderness between men and men as part of our democratic heritage, part of the adhesiveness which would make the democracy function; that men could work together not as competitive beasts but as tender lovers and fellows. So he projected from his own desire and from his own unconsciousness a sexual urge he felt was normal to the unconscious of most people, though forbidden, for the most part, to take part. Walt Whitman is one of my spiritual teachers and I am following him in this poem taking off from a line of his own and projecting my own actual unconsciousness feeling of which I don't have shame, sir, which I feel are basically charming, actually.

THE COURT: I didn't hear that last word.

THE WITNESS: Charming

MR. FORAN: I have no further questions

THE COURT: Redirect examination. Nothing? You may go sir.

THE WITNESS: Thank you.

THE COURT: Call your next witness.

# Testimony Of Timothy Leary

THE COURT: Will you call the witness, please?

MR. KUNSTLER: Would you state your full name for the record?

THE WITNESS: Timothy F. Leary.

MR. KUNSTLER: Dr. Leary, what is your present occupation?

THE WITNESS: I am the Democratic candidate for Governor in California.

MR. KUNSTLER: Is that in the primary?

THE WITNESS: Yes, sir, Democratic primary

THE COURT: Just so that the jury will be clear, do you call being a candidate an occupation, sir?

THE WITNESS: Well, it is taking most of my time at present, your Honor.

THE COURT: What is your regular occupation?

THE WITNESS: I am a religious ordained minister, and I am a college lecturer.

MR. KUNSTLER: Can you state what your educational background is?

THE WITNESS: Yes, sir, I received a Ph.D. in clinical psychology from the University of California, Berkeley, in 1950. I was two years at Holy Cross College, and a year and a half at West Point, the United States Military Academy.

MR. KUNSTLER: Now, Dr. Leary, can you state briefly your professional experience since receiving your Ph.D. in 1950?

THE WITNESS: Yes, from 1950 to 1956, I was on the faculty of the University of California and the University of California Medical School in San Francisco. I was also the director of the Kaiser Foundation Psychological Research from 1952 to 1957.

MR. KUNSTLER: And after that?

THE WITNESS: I taught at the University of Copenhagen in the Philosophy and Psychology Department in Denmark in 1958, and then in 1959 I joined the faculty at Harvard University and taught at Harvard from 1959 to 1963 in clinical psychology and personality psychology.

MR. KUNSTLER: Dr. Leary, have you been the author of any publications?

THE WITNESS: Yes, I have written two books on experimental clinical psychology and about twenty scientific articles in this field. I have written six books and over fifty scientific articles on the effects of psychedelic drugs on human psychology and human consciousness.

MR. KUNSTLER: Doctor, can you explain what a psychedelic drug is?

THE WITNESS: I will try. Psychedelic drugs are drugs which speed up thinking, which broaden the consciousness, which produce religious experiences or creative experiences, or philosophic experiences in the person who takes them. These psychedelic drugs, of course, are the opposite of the nonpsychedelic drugs like heroin, or alcohol, and barbiturates which slow down thinking, as opposed to psychedelic drugs which expand and accelerate the consciousness.

MR. KUNSTLER: Now, there came a time, did there not, Dr. Leary, when you left Harvard University?

THE WITNESS: Yes, I was dismissed from Harvard University in 1963. There were two reasons for my dismissal. One was a dispute over schedule of classes, and the other was because I was continuing to do research on the effects of psychedelic drugs which was politically risky for Harvard University to sponsor.

MR. KUNSTLER: What was the nature of that research?

MR. FORAN: I object to that, your Honor.

THE COURT: I sustain the objection.

MR. KUNSTLER: Your Honor, we want to show the background of Dr. Leary and the type of work he was doing. There has been a great misconception about the type of work he was doing. We want to explain it to the jury.

THE COURT: Dr. Leary's work isn't in issue here. He is not a defendant here.

MR. KUNSTLER: Now, Dr. Leary, do you recall when your first met Jerry Rubin?

THE WITNESS: Yes, I do. I met Jerry Rubin at the love-in at San Francisco, which was January 1967.

MR. KUNSTLER: And do you know where that love-in was held?

THE WITNESS: Yes, that was held in Golden Gate Park, and I think either seventy or eighty thousand people came to the park to participate in this love-in.

MR. FORAN: Objection.

THE COURT: I sustain the objection. Seven or eight thousand?

MR. KUNSTLER: Seventy or eighty thousand.

THE COURT: Oh, even worse.

MR. KUNSTLER: Even better. All right, Dr. Leary, when did you first meet Abbie Hoffman?

THE WITNESS: The first time I met Mr. Hoffman was at the LSD Shrine and Rescue Center in New York City. That would be November or December of 1966.

MR. KUNSTLER: Now, lest there be any confusion, what does LSD stand for?

THE WITNESS: It was the League of Spiritual Discovery. That was a religion incorporated in the State of New York and we had a rescue center in New York where hundreds of people taking drugs could be rehabilitated.

MR. KUNSTLER: Dr. Leary, I call your attention to late January of 1968 and ask you whether you met with Jerry and Abbie during that month at that time?

THE WITNESS: Yes, I did. I met with Mr. Hoffman and Mr. Rubin and with other people and we formed and founded the Youth International Party.

MR. KUNSTLER: Now, with reference to the founding of the Youth International Party, which we will refer to as Yippie, can you state what was said by the people attending there with reference to the founding of this party?

THE WITNESS: Well, Julius Lester said that the current parties are not responsive to the needs of black people, particularly young black people. Allen Ginsberg said that the Democrat and Republican Parties are not responsive to the creative youth and to college students and high school students who expect more from society. Abbie Hoffman, as I remember, was particularly eloquent in describing the need for new political tactics and techniques.

MR. FORAN: Objection.

THE COURT: You are not privileged to characterize the participants in that way.

MR. KUNSTLER: Even if you were impressed by what people said, don't indicate whether they were eloquent or what-have-you.

MR. FORAN: Your Honor, I object to Mr. Kunstler's comments which he knows are improper.

MR. KUNSTLER: I was trying to assist Mr. Foran.

THE COURT: I will do the directing. You ask the questions.

MR. KUNSTLER: Would you go ahead, Dr. Leary?

THE WITNESS: Abbie Hoffman said that new political methods were needed because the conventions of the Democrat and Republican Parties were controlled by machine politics which had nothing to do with the needs of the people.

Mr. Hoffman continued to say that we should set up a series of political meetings throughout the country, not just for the coming summer but for the coming years. Mr. Hoffman suggested that we have love-ins or be-ins in which thousands of young people and freedom-loving people throughout the country could get together on Sunday afternoons, listen to music which represented the new point of view, the music of love and peace and harmony, and try to bring about a political change in this country that would be nonviolent in people's minds and in their hearts, and this is the concept of the love-in which Mr. Hoffman was urging upon us.

MR. KUNSTLER: Now, at any time during this discussion did anyone make an reference to the Democratic National Convention?

THE WITNESS: Mr. Hoffman said it was important to have a large group of young people and black people and freedom-loving people come to Chicago during the Democratic Convention the following August. That it was important that people that were concerned about peace and brotherhood, come to Chicago and in a very dignified, beautiful way meet in the parks and represent what Mr. Hoffman called the politics of life and politics of love and peace and brotherhood. Mr. Rubin, I remember, pointed out that since the Democratic Party was meeting here, there was great concern about having police and having National Guard and they were bringing in tear gas. Mr. Rubin pointed out that it could possibly be violent here, and both Mr. Rubin and Allen Ginsberg said that they didn't think that we should come to Chicago if there was a possibility of violence from the soldiers or the police.

MR. KUNSTLER: I call your attention to March of 1968, somewhere in the middle of March, and I ask you if you can recall being present at a press conference?

THE WITNESS: Yes.

MR. KUNSTLER: Prior to this press conference had you had any other meetings with Jerry and Abbie?

THE WITNESS: Yes, we had met two or three times during the spring.

MR. FORAN: Your Honor, I object to the constant use of the diminutives in the reference to the defendants.

MR. KUNSTLER: Your Honor, sometimes it is hard because we work together in this case, we use first names constantly.

THE COURT: I know, but if I knew you that well, and I don't, how would it seem for me to say, "Now, Billy — "

MR. KUNSTLER: Your Honor, it is perfectly acceptable to me — if I could have the reverse privilege.

THE COURT: I don't like it. I have disapproved of it before and I ask you now to refer to the defendants by their surnames.

MR. KUNSTLER: I was just thinking I hadn't been called "Billy" since my mother used that word the first time.

THE COURT: I haven't called you that.

MR. KUNSTLER: It evokes some memories.

THE COURT: I was trying to point out to you how absurd it sounds in a courtroom.

MR. KUNSTLER: Dr. Leary, did you speak at that press conference?

THE WITNESS: Yes. I described in great detail the harassment that we had suffered in our religious center at Millbrook, New York, by the police. I describe how for the preceding two or three months there had been a police blockade around this young people's center in upstate New York and that our houses had been ransacked at night by sheriffs and policemen and how our young children were being arrested on their bicycles on the roads outside of our houses because they didn't have identification. And I described how helicopters had been coming over to observe our behavior and I raised the possibility that we did not want this to happen in Chicago and we hoped that Chicago would be free from this sort of unpleasant encounter, because at Millbrook we were living very peaceably, bothering nobody until we were harassed and surrounded by the police.

MR. KUNSTLER: Now, during the month of March did you have occasion to speak with Jerry Rubin?

THE WITNESS: Yes, I called Jerry to tell him about the results of the Yippie meeting in Chicago.

MR. KUNSTLER: All right. Will you tell the jury and the Court what you told Jerry and what he told you, if anything, in that phone conversation?

THE WITNESS: I told Mr. Rubin that I had never experienced such fear on the part of the young people as I did in the young people of Chicago, that they were, literally trembling about the possibility of violence in August. And I raised the issue to Jerry as to whether we should reconsider coming to Chicago.

MR. KUNSTLER: Now, up to this time in this telephone conversation had you had any conversation with Jerry Rubin or Abbie Hoffman about LSD in the Chicago water supply?

MR. FORAN: I object to that, your Honor.

THE COURT: I sustain the objection.

MR. KUNSTLER: Now, Dr. Leary, I call your attention to April of 1968. and ask you if you recall a meeting with Jerry Rubin and Abbie Hoffman?

THE WITNESS: Yes, I met with Jerry Rubin and Abbie Hoffman.

MR. KUNSTLER: What did you say?

THE WITNESS: Mr. Hoffman pointed out that since our last meeting, President Johnson had retired from office. Therefore, President Johnson would not be coming to Chicago. Therefore, the meaning of a celebration of life on our part as opposed to Mr. Johnson was lost since the man we were attempting to oppose was not going to come to Chicago. Both Mr. Hoffman and Mr. Rubin at that time said to me before I left that they were not sure whether we should come to Chicago, and that we would watch what happened politically. At that time, Jerry Rubin pointed out that Robert Kennedy was still alive, and many of us felt that he represented the aspirations of young people, so we thought we would wait. I remember Mr. Rubin saving, "Let's wait and see what Robert Kennedy comes out with as far as peace is concerned. Let's wait to see if Robert Kennedy does speak to voting people, and if Robert Kennedy does seek to represent the peaceful, joyous, erotic feelings of young people—"

THE COURT: "Erotic," did you say?

THE WITNESS: Erotic.

THE COURT: E-R-O-T-I-C?

THE WITNESS: Eros. That means love, your Honor.

THE COURT: I know, I know. I wanted to be sure I didn't mishear you.

THE WITNESS: So Mr. Rubin suggested that we hold off the decision as to whether we come to Chicago until we saw how Mr. Kennedy's campaign developed, and at that point, I think most of us would have gladly, joyously called off the Chicago meeting.

MR. KUNSTLER: You did not yourself come to Chicago, did you, during the Democratic National Convention?

THE WITNESS: No. I did not come to Chicago myself.

MR. KUNSTLER: Right. Now prior to the Convention week, did you have any conversation with Jerry Rubin?

THE WITNESS: Yes, at the end of July. I told Mr. Rubin that I had decided not to come to Chicago. Mr. Rubin asked me why.

MR. FORAN: Objection as to his reasons for not coming.

THE COURT: I should say that is irrelevant. I sustain the objection.

MR. KUNSTLER: Your witness.

THE COURT: Cross-examination.

MR. FORAN: Dr. Leary, will you name the drugs that you said speeded up thinking?

THE WITNESS: Yes, psychedelic or mind-expanding drugs include LSD, mescaline, peyote, marijuana, and I could go on. There is a list of perhaps thirty or forty chemical compounds and natural vines and herbs. Do you want more?

MR. FORAN: No, that is enough.

Now, when you talked to Jerry Rubin in late March over the telephone from Chicago, you had a long discussion with him at that time about your fears of violence that would occur in Chicago at the Democratic Convention, did you not?

THE WITNESS: Yes, I had been told this by the young people in Chicago.

MR. FORAN: And you expressed your concern?

THE WITNESS: Well, I am always concerned about the possibility of violence anywhere at any time. I am against violence.

MR. FORAN: You asked him at that time whether or not you should reconsider coming to Chicago, is that correct?

THE WITNESS: Yes, sir.

MR. FORAN: I have no further questions.

MR. KUNSTLER: I have just one further question. Dr. Leary, in answer to Mr. Foran's question about the young people, did you tell Jerry Rubin from where the young people in Chicago expected violence to come, from what source?

THE WITNESS: Well, from the militia, the National Guard. The sheriff was fighting with the police chief of Chicago at the time, and the sheriff, I believe, was enlisting vigilantes and just people off the street to be deputy sheriffs.

MR. KUNSTLER: But it was violence from the police?

THE WITNESS: And the National Guard, police, and sheriff.

MR. KUNSTLER: And not from the young people themselves?

THE WITNESS: There was no possibility of that.

MR. KUNSTLER: Thank you.

THE COURT: No further questions? You may go.

# Testimony Of Norman Mailer

MR. KUNSTLER: Would you state your full name, please?

THE WITNESS: Norman Mailer is my full name. I was born Norman Kingsley Mailer, but I don't use the middle name.

MR. KUNSTLER: Would you state, Mr. Mailer, what your occupation is?

THE WITNESS: I am a writer.

MR. KUNSTLER: I show you D-344 for identification and ask you if you can identify this book.

THE WITNESS: This a book written by me about the march on the Pentagon and its title is *The Armies of the Night*.

MR. KUNSTLER: Can you state whether or not this book won the Pulitzer Prize?

THE WITNESS: It did.

MR. SCHULTZ: Objection.

THE COURT: I sustain the objection. I strike the witness' answer and I direct the jury to disregard it.

MR. KUNSTLER: Can you state what awards this book has won?

THE WITNESS: The book was awarded the National Book Award and the Pulitzer Prize in 1969.

MR. KUNSTLER: I call your attention, Mr. Mailer, to—let me withdraw that. Did you have a conversation with Jerry Rubin after the Pentagon?

THE WITNESS: Yes, I did in December in my home. I had called Mr. Rubin and asked him to see me because I was writing an account of the march on the Pentagon. I was getting in touch with those principals whom I could locate. Mr. Rubin was, if you will, my best witness. We talked about the details of the march on the Pentagon for hours. We went into great detail about many aspects of it. And in this period I formed a very good opinion of Mr. Rubin because he had extraordinary powers of objectivity which an author is greatly in need of when he is talking to witnesses.

MR. SCHULTZ: Your Honor—Mr. Mailer—

THE COURT: I will have to strike the witness' answer and direct the jury to disregard every word of it.

MR. SCHULTZ: Your Honor, would you instruct Mr. Mailer even though he can't use all of the adjectives which he uses in his work, he should say "he said" and "I said," or if he wants to embellish that, then "I stated" and "he stated." But that's the way it is related before a jury.

THE COURT: We are simple folk here. All you have to do is say "he said", if anything, "I said," if anything, and if your wife said something, you may say what she said. I strike the witness' answer, as I say, and I direct the jury to disregard it.

MR. KUNSTLER: Now, was anything said in the conversation about what happened at the Pentagon?

THE WITNESS: Mr. Rubin went into considerable detail about his view of the American military effort in Vietnam and the structure of the military and industrial establishment in America, and it was in Mr. Rubin's view—

MR. SCHULTZ: Your Honor, could he state what Mr. Rubin said relating to what he observed at the Pentagon?

THE WITNESS: This is Mr. Rubin's view. Mr. Rubin said it was his view, Counselor, he said that military-industrial establishment was so full of guilt and so horrified secretly at what they were doing in Vietnam that they were ready to crack at the smallest sort of provocation, and that the main idea in the move on the Pentagon was to exacerbate their sense of authority and control.

MR. KUNSTLER: Mr. Mailer, was anything said about Chicago in this conversation?

THE WITNESS: Yes. Mr. Rubin said that he was at present working full time on plans to have a youth festival in Chicago in August of 1968 when the Democratic Convention would take place and it was his idea that the presence of a hundred thousand young people in Chicago at a festival with rock bands would so intimidate and terrify the establishment that Lyndon Johnson would have to be nominated under armed guard. And I said, "Wow." I was overtaken with the audacity of the idea and I said, "It's a beautiful and frightening idea." And Rubin said, "I think that the beauty of it is that the establishment is going to do it all themselves. We won't do a thing. We are just going to be there and they won't be able to take it. They will smash the city themselves. They will provoke all the violence." And I said, "I think you're right, but I have to admit to you that I'm scared at the thought of it. It is really something." And he said, "It is. I am going to devote full time to it." I said, "You're a brave man."

MR. KUNSTLER: Now did you go to Chicago?

THE WITNESS: Yes.

MR. KUNSTLER: I call your attention to approximately 5:00 p.m. on August 27, 1968. Do you know where you were then?

THE WITNESS: Yes. I was in my hotel room with Robert Lowell and David Dellinger and Rennie Davis.

MR. KUNSTLER: Would you state what was said during that conversation?

THE WITNESS: The conversation was about the possibility of violence on a march that was being proposed to the Amphitheatre. Mr. Lowell and I were a little worried about it because we were McCarthy supporters and we felt that if there was a lot of violence it was going to wash out McCarthy's last remote chance of being nominated. And Mr. Dellinger said to me, "Look, you know my record, you know I've never had anything to do with violence." He said, "And you know that we have not been the violent ones. For every policeman that has been called a pig, those police have broken five and ten heads. You know that I never move toward anything that will result in violence," he said, "but at the same time I am not going to avoid all activity which could possible result in violence because if we do that, we'll be able to protest nothing at all. We are trying at this very moment to get a permit, we are hoping we get the permit, but if they don't give it to us, we'll probably march anyway because we have to: it's why we're here. We're here to oppose the war in Vietnam and we don't protest it if we stay in our rooms and don't go out to protest it." He then asked me to speak at Grant Park the next day.

MR. KUNSTLER: Did you accept that invitation?

THE WITNESS: No, I didn't. I said I was there to cover the Convention for *Harper's* Magazine, and I felt that I did not want to get involved because if I did and got arrested, I would not be able to write my piece in time for the deadline, and I was really very concerned about not getting arrested, and losing three, or four, or five days because I had eighteen days in which to write the piece, and I knew it was going to be a long piece.

MR. KUNSTLER: I call your attention to the next day, Wednesday, the twenty-eighth of August, between 3:30 and 4:00 p.m. approximately. Do you know where you were then?

THE WITNESS: Yes, I was in Grant Park. I felt ashamed of myself for not speaking, and I, therefore, went up to the platform and I asked Mr. Dellinger if I could speak, and he then very happily said, "Yes, of course."

MR. KUNSTLER: Can you state what you did say on Wednesday in Grant Park?

THE WITNESS: I merely said to the people who were there that I thought they were possessed of beauty, and that I was not going to march with them because I had to write this piece. And they all said, "Write, Baby." That is what they said from the crowd.

MR. KUNSTLER: Now, Mr. Mailer, I call your attention to Thursday, August 29, did you give another speech that day?

THE WITNESS: Yes, that was in Grant Park on Thursday morning, two or three in the morning.

MR. KUNSTLER: Do you recall what you said?

THE WITNESS: Yes. That was—

MR. SCHULTZ: Objection. What he said is not relevant. What he said at the Bandshell where the Bandshell performance was sponsored by the defendants, that is one thing, but where he makes an independent statement—

THE COURT: There hasn't been a proper foundation for the question.

MR. KUNSTLER: I will ask one question.

THE COURT: I sustain the objection.

MR. KUNSTLER: Mr. Mailer, at the time you spoke, did you see any of the defendants at this table in the vicinity?

THE WITNESS: No, I don't think so.

MR. KUNSTLER: Then I have no further questions.

THE COURT: Is there any cross-examination?

MR. SCHULTZ: A few questions, your Honor. Mr. Mailer, when you had your conversation with Rubin at your home, did Rubin tell you that the presence of a hundred thousand young people would so intimidate the establishment that Johnson would have to call out the troops and National Guard?

THE WITNESS: He did not use the word intimidate, as I recollect.

MR. SCHULTZ: Did he say that the presence of these people will provoke the establishment and the establishment will smash the city themselves?

THE WITNESS: That was the substance of what he said, yes.

MR. SCHULTZ: All right. Now at your speech in Grant Park, didn't you say that we are at the beginning of a war which would continue for twenty years and the march today would be one battle in that war?

THE WITNESS: Yes, I said that.

MR. SCHULTZ: But you couldn't go on the march because you had a deadline?

THE WITNESS: Yes. I was in a moral quandary. I didn't know if I was being scared or being professional and I was naturally quite upset because a man never likes to know that his motive might be simple fear.

THE COURT: I thought you said you had to do that piece.

THE WITNESS: I did have to do the piece, your Honor, but I just wasn't sure in my own mind whether I was hiding behind the piece or whether I was being professional to avoid temptation.

MR. SCHULTZ: Did you tell the crowd, Mr. Mailer, at the Bandshell, "You have to be beautiful. You are much better than you were at the Pentagon?" Did you tell them that?

THE WITNESS: Yes. I remember saying that.

MR. SCHULTZ: You were talking about their physical appearance rather than their actions?

THE WITNESS: That is right. To my amazement these militant activities seemed to improve their physique and their features.

MR. SCHULTZ: I have no further questions.

THE COURT: Is there any redirect examination?

MR. KUNSTLER: Could you state if Rubin didn't use the word "intimidate" as you have answered Mr. Schultz, what word he did use? What was his language?

THE WITNESS: It would be impossible for me to begin to remember whether Mr. Rubin used the word "intimidate" or not. I suspect that he probably did not use it because it is not his habitual style of speech. He would speak more of diverting, demoralizing the establishment, freaking them out, bending their mind, driving them out of their bird.

I use the word "intimidate" because possibly since I am a bully by nature, I tend to think in terms of intimidation, but I don't think Mr. Rubin does. He thinks in terms of cataclysm, of having people reveal their own guilt, their own evil.

His whole notion was that the innocent presence of one hundred thousand people in Chicago would be intolerable for a man as guilt-ridden as Lyndon Johnson. When this conversation took place, Lyndon Johnson was still President and the war in Vietnam gave no sign of ever being diminished in its force and its waste.

MR. KUNSTLER: I have no further questions.

# Testimony Of Judy Collins

MR. KUNSTLER: Would you state your name, please?

THE WITNESS: Judy Collins.

MR. KUNSTLER: What is your occupation?

THE WITNESS: I'm a singer. I sing folksongs.

MR. KUNSTLER: Now, Miss Collins, I call your attention to March 17 of 1968 at approximately noontime on that date. Do you know where you were?

THE WITNESS: I was at the Americana Hotel in New York City attending a press conference to announce the formation of what we have now come to know of as the Yippie Movement.

MR. KUNSTLER: Who was present at that press conference?

THE WITNESS: There were a number of people who were singers, entertainers. Jerry Rubin was there, Abbie Hoffman was there. Allen Ginsberg was there, and sang a mantra.

MR. KUNSTLER: Now what did you do at that press conference?

THE WITNESS: Well—[*sings*] "Where have all the flowers—

THE COURT: Just a minute, young lady.

THE WITNESS: [*sings*] " — where have all the flowers gone?"

DEPUTY MARSHAL JOHN J. GRACIOUS: I'm sorry. The Judge would like to speak to you.

THE COURT: We don't allow any singing in this Court. I'm sorry.

THE WITNESS: May I recite the words?

MR. KUNSTLER: Well, your Honor, we have had films. I think it is as legitimate as a movie. It is the actual thing she did, she sang "Where Have All the Flowers Gone," which is a well-known peace song, and she sang it, and the jury is not getting the flavor.

THE COURT: You asked her what she did, and she proceeded to sing.

MR. KUNSTLER: That is what she did, your Honor.

THE WITNESS: That's what I do.

THE COURT: And that has no place in a United States District Court. We are not here to be entertained, sir. We are trying a very important case.

MR. KUNSTLER: This song is not an entertainment, your Honor. This is a song of peace, and what happens to young men and women during wartime.

THE COURT: I forbid her from singing during the trial. I will not permit singing in this Courtroom.

MR. KUNSTLER: Why not, your Honor? What's wrong with singing?

MR. FORAN: May I respond? This is about the fifth time this has occurred. Each time your Honor has directed Mr. Kunstler that it was improper in the courtroom. It is an old and stale joke in this Courtroom, your Honor. Now, there is no question that Miss Collins is a fine singer. In my family my six kids and I all agree that she is a fine singer, but that doesn't have a thing to do with this lawsuit nor what my profession is, which is the practice of law in the Federal District Court, your Honor, and I protest Mr. Kunstler constantly failing to advise his witnesses of what proper decorum is, and I object to it on behalf of the Government.

THE COURT: I sustain the objection.

MR. KUNSTLER: What did you say at the press conference?

THE WITNESS: I said a great deal. I said I want to see a celebration of life, not of destruction. I said that my soul and my profession and my life has become part of a movement toward hopefully removing the causes for death, the causes for war, the causes for the prevalence of violence in our society, and in order to make my voice heard, I said that I would indeed come to Chicago and that I would sing. That is what I do, that's my profession. I said that I was there because life was the force that I wished to make my songs and mv life known for. I said that I would be in Chicago with thousands of people who want to celebrate life, and I said these words, in the context of a song. I said:


"Where have all the flowers gone?  Long time passing.
Where have all the flowers gone?  Long time ago.
Where have all the flowers gone?  Young girls have picked them, every one.
 Oh, when will they ever learn?
Where have all the young girls gone?  Long time passing.
Where have all the young girls gone?  Long time ago.
Where have all the young girls gone?  Gone for husbands, every one.
Oh, when will they ever learn?
Where have all the young men gone?  Long time passing.
Where have all the young men gone?  Long time ago.
Where have all the young men gone?  Gone for soldiers, every one.
When will they ever learn?
Where have all the soldiers gone?  Long time passing
Where have all the soldiers gone?  Long time ago.
Where have all the soldiers gone?  Gone to graveyards, every one.
Oh, when will they ever learn?"

I said that I would give my music and my voice to a situation in which people could express themselves about life, with a permit, of course, from the City of Chicago.

MR. KUNSTLER: Now, I call your attention, Miss Collins, to the last or next to last day of April of 1968, did you have an occasion to see Abbie Hoffman on that day?

THE WITNESS: Yes. We met at my house. Abbie Hoffman said that there was a lot of trouble in Chicago getting the permits. I said that I felt if the City of Chicago wanted to provoke violence and wanted to provoke unrest, all they had to do was continue ignoring our requests for grants and also continue the kind of things that had been happening. Daley had just said that he would shoot to kill, and I told Abbie that I was not encouraged by that attitude on the part of the City of Chicago and that I felt that they should further their efforts to get the permits for us to appear. Abbie Hoffman said that the National Guard was going to be brought in, and I told him at that point that if it was possible, I'd like to arrange to perform and sing also for the National Guard, as they would be there under duress, and they should hear what we all had to say.

MR. KUNSTLER: Now, I call your attention to the third week in June of 1968. Did you have an occasion to have a conversation with Rennie Davis?

THE WITNESS: Yes. Rennie Davis called me, and asked me if I had any desire to join a group of people who were trying to set up coffee houses which would be hosts to GI's all over the country. He invited me to come to Fort Hood. I told him that I felt that since the USO provides entertainment of a certain kind to GI's, that I would be very willing to go to an installation, a base, and perform at a coffee house to expose the GI's there to my point of view, to the young people's point of view, and to our attempts to create a life force, and to also express to the GI's that we're on their side. We don't want them to die. We don't want them to be exposed to the kind of terror that war will perpetrate.

MR. FORAN: I object, your Honor, as to relevancy. There is no relevancy.

MR. KUNSTLER: Your Honor, the lives and deaths of American soldiers I think is highly relevant. It was the whole purpose or one of the main purposes people came to Chicago.

THE COURT: Life and death are really very wonderful. This is a great place to live in and be alive. I agree with you. But those things are not an issue in this case.

MR. KUNSTLER: Miss Collins, I call your attention to approximately one week before the opening of the convention, the week of August 19, 1968. Did you have an occasion to talk to Abbie Hoffman?

THE WITNESS: Yes. In fact, Abbie did call me to ask me again whether I would participate in the Yippie Celebration of Life.

MR. KUNSTLER: Now, would you relate what he said to you and what you said to him?

THE WITNESS: Well, Abbie told me that what was happening in Chicago was that the police were acting antagonistically towards peace demonstrations. He wanted to warn me that I would be subject to that same kind of provocation as an entertainer performing in a public place without a permit. I told him that I was frightened, now that I had seen things on television that were disturbing to me and upsetting to me, that I had heard Mayor Daley's declaration of war on me personally. I said, "Abbie, you must continue to try in every way possible to get those permits, because if we're going to have a celebration, we must do it legally. I don't want to be violent. I'm not going to Chicago to do anything except sing for people in a legal situation." Abbie asked if I was sure that I wouldn't come if they couldn't get permits because they didn't know if they could or not. And I said that it was doubtful, that I would have to think about it, but as far as my wellbeing went and as far as the wellbeing of all the people that I feel I represent went, that I could not put myself in a position to jeopardize my physical wellbeing or those of thousands of other young people who would be there to celebrate with us.

MR. KUNSTLER: Did you go to Chicago during Convention week?

THE WITNESS: No, I did not. I stayed away from Chicago because the permits were not granted.

MR. KUNSTLER: And anything that was planned, or generated, or that might cause or be a participating factor in violent activity, you wouldn't want anything to do with it, would you?

THE WITNESS: There was nothing violent about anything that went on in the preparations on our side for this Convention. We were provoked.

MR. KUNSTLER: No further questions.

THE COURT: Cross-examination.

\* \* \* \* \* \* \* \* \*

MR. FORAN: Miss Collins, you said in your meeting in April with Mr. Hoffman, didn't you testify that Mr. Hoffman told you that they had been trying to get permits for months in Chicago?

THE WITNESS: Yes, they had been attempting to get permits.

MR. FORAN: This is what he told you.

THE WITNESS: Yes, I knew this was a fact. This wasn't only Abbie Hoffman speaking. This was—

THE COURT: That will be all.

THE WITNESS: That was the consensus that had been going on.

THE COURT: Will you, young lady—

THE WITNESS: There was a refusal to grant it.

THE COURT: Do you hear very well? Do you want to move your hair back?

THE WITNESS: I think so, yes.

THE COURT: I want to ask you, I want to tell you that you have answered the question, you may not go beyond that.

THE WITNESS: Oh, well, I assumed that he wanted to hear more about what statement—

MR. FORAN: Did you know that only one permit had been filed for?

THE WITNESS: I believe that was what I knew then.

MR. FORAN: Did you know that it hadn't been turned down yet?

THE WITNESS: Well it had not been granted. It had been applied for for months.

MR. FORAN: Miss Collins, did Mr. Hoffman tell you that he was planning to tear up Lincoln Park in the city of Chicago?

THE WITNESS: No, I don't believe he ever said that to me. No, I don't think so.

MR. FORAN: I don't think he would tell it to you either.

THE WITNESS: I told him I was going to create an exciting environment with my music, but he didn't say he was going to tear up Grant Park, no.

MR. FORAN: Did Mr. Hoffman tell you that he had come to Chicago prepared to die if necessary to open the city of Chicago up? Did he tell you that?

THE WITNESS: I don't remember that he ever said those exact words.

MR. FORAN: I don't have anything further.

# Closing Argument for the Defendants

MR. KUNSTLER: Ladies and Gentlemen of the jury:

This is the last voice that you will hear from the defense. We have no rebuttal. This Government has the last word.

In an introductory fashion I would just like to state that only you will judge this case as far as the facts go. This is your solemn responsibility and it is an awesome one.

After you have heard Mr. Schultz and Mr. Weinglass, there must be lots of questions running in your minds. You have seen the same scenes described by two different people. You have heard different interpretations of those scenes by two different people. But you are the ones that draw the final inference. You will be the ultimate arbiters of the fate of these seven men.

In deciding this case we are relying upon your oath of office and that you will decide it only on the facts, not on whether you like the lawyers or don't like the lawyers. We are really quite unimportant. Whether you like the judge or don't like the judge, that is unimportant, too. Whether you like the defendants or don't like the defendants —

THE COURT: I am glad you didn't say I was unimportant.

MR. KUNSTLER: No. The likes or dislikes are unimportant.

And I can say that it is not whether you like the defendants or don't like the defendants. You may detest all of the defendants, for all I know; you may love all of them, I don't know. It is unimportant. It shouldn't interfere with your decision, it shouldn't come into it. And this is hard to do. You have seen a long defense here. There have been harsh things said in this court, and harsh things to look at from your jury box. You have seen a man bound and gagged. You have heard lots of things which are probably all not pleasant. Some of them have been humorous. Some have been bitter. Some may have been downright boring, and I imagine many were. Those things really shouldn't influence your decision. You have an oath to decide the facts and to decide them divorced of any personal considerations of your own, and I remind you that if you don't do that, you will be living a lie the rest of your life, and only you will be living with that lie.

Now, I don't think it has been any secret to you that the defendants have some questions as to whether they are receiving a fair trial. That has been raised many times.

MR. FORAN: Your Honor, I object to this.

THE COURT: I sustain the objection.

MR. KUNSTLER: They stand here indicted under a new statute. In fact, the conspiracy, which is Count I, starts the day after the President signed the law.

MR. FORAN: Your Honor, I object to that. The law is for the Court to determine, not for counsel to determine.

THE COURT: I sustain the objection.

MR. KUNSTLER: Your Honor, I am not going into the law. They have a right to know when it was passed.

THE COURT: I don't want my responsibility usurped by you.

MR. KUNSTLER: I want you to know, first that these defendants had a constitutional right to travel. They have a constitutional right to dissent and to agitate for dissent. No one would deny that, not Mr. Foran, and not I, or anyone else.

Just some fifty years ago, I think almost exactly, in a criminal court building here in Chicago, Clarence Darrow said this:

"When a new truth comes upon the earth, or a great idea necessary for mankind is born, where does it come from? Not from the police force, or the prosecuting attorneys, or the judges, or the lawyers, or the doctors. Not there. It comes from the despised and the outcasts, and it comes perhaps from jails and prisons. It comes from men who have dared to be rebels and think their thoughts, and their faith has been the faith of rebels.

"What do you suppose would have happened to the working men except for these rebels all the way down through history? Think of the complacent cowardly people who never raise their voices against the powers that be. If there had been only these, you gentlemen of the jury would be hewers of wood and drawers of water. You gentlemen would have been slaves. You gentlemen owe whatever you have and whatever you hope to these brave rebels who dared to think, and dared to speak, and dared to act."

This was Clarence Darrow fifty years ago in another case.

You don't have to look for rebels in other countries. You can just look at the history of this country.

You will recall that there was a great demonstration that took place around the Custom House in Boston in 1770. It was a demonstration of the people of Boston against the people who were enforcing the Sugar Act, the Stamp Act, the Quartering of Troops Act. And they picketed at one place where it was important to be, at the Custom House where the customs were collected.

You remember the testimony in this case. Superintendent Rochford said, "Go up to Lincoln Park, go to the Bandshell, go anywhere you want, but don't go to the Amphitheatre."

That was like telling the Boston patriots, "Go anywhere you want, but don't go to the Custom House," because it was at the Custom House and it was at the Amphitheatre that the protesters wanted to show that something was terribly and totally wrong. They wanted to show it at the place it was important, and so the seeming compliance of the City in saying "Go anywhere you want throughout the city. Go to Jackson Park. Go to Lincoln Park," has no meaning. That is an excuse for preventing a demonstration at the single place that had meaning, which was the Amphitheatre.

The Custom House in Boston was the scene of evil and so the patriots demonstrated. They ran into a Chicago. You know what happened. The British soldiers shot them down and killed five of them, including one black man, Crispus Attucks, who was the first man to die, by the way, in the American revolution. They were shot down in the street by the British for demonstrating at the Custom House.

You will remember that after the Boston Massacre, which was the name the Colonies gave to it, all sorts of things happened in the Colonies. There were all sorts of demonstrations —

MR. FORAN: Your Honor, I have sat here quite a while and I object to this. This is not a history lecture. The purpose of summation is to sum up the facts of the case and I object to this.

THE COURT: I do sustain the objection. Unless you get down to evidence, I will direct you to discontinue this lecture on history. We are not dealing with history.

MR. KUNSTLER: But to understand the overriding issues as well, your Honor —

THE COURT: I will not permit any more of these historical references and I direct you to discontinue them, sir.

MR. KUNSTLER: I do so under protest, your Honor. I will get down, because the judge has prevented me from going into material that I wanted to —

MR. FORAN: Your Honor, I object to that comment.

THE COURT: I have not prevented you. I have ruled properly as a matter of law. The law prevents you from doing it, sir.

MR. KUNSTLER: I will get down to the evidence in this case. I am going to confine my remarks to showing you how the Government stoops to conquer in this case.

The prosecution recognized early that if you were to see thirty-three police officers in uniform take the stand that you would realize how much of the case depends on law enforcement officers. So they strip the uniforms from those witnesses, and you notice you began to see almost an absence of uniforms. Even the Deputy Police Chief came without a uniform.

Mr. Schultz said, "Look at our witnesses. They don't argue with the judge. They are bright and alert. They sit there and they answer clearly."

They answered like automatons — one after the other, robots took the stand. "Did you see any missiles?"

"A barrage."

Everybody saw a barrage of missiles.

"What were the demonstrators doing?"

"Screaming. Indescribably loud."

"What were they screaming?"

"Profanities of all sorts."

I call your attention to James Murray. That is the reporter, and this is the one they got caught with. This is the one that slipped up. James Murray, who is a friend of the police, who thinks the police are the steadying force in Chicago. This man came to the stand, and he wanted you to rise up when you heard "Viet Cong flags," this undeclared war we are fighting against an undeclared enemy. He wanted you to think that the march from Grant Park into the center of Chicago in front of the Conrad Hilton was a march run by the Viet Cong, or have the Viet Cong flags so infuriate you that you would feel against these demonstrators that they were less than human beings. The only problem is that he never saw any Viet-Cong flags. First of all, there were none, and I call your attention to the movies, and if you see one Viet Cong flag in those two hours of movies at Michigan and Balbo, you can call me a liar and convict my clients.

Mr. Murray, under whatever instructions were given to him, or under his own desire to help the Police Department, saw them. I asked him a simple question: describe them. Remember what he said? "They are black." Then he heard laughter in the courtroom because there isn't a person in the room that thinks the Viet Cong flag is a black flag. He heard a twitter in the courtroom. He said, "No, they are red."

Then he heard a little more laughter.

Then I said, "Are they all red?"

He said, "No, they have some sort of a symbol on them."

"What is the symbol?"

"I can't remember."

When you look at the pictures, you won't even see any black flags at Michigan and Balbo. You will see some red flags, two of them, I believe, and I might say to you that a red flag was the flag under which General Washington fought at the Battle of Brandywine, a flag made for him by the nuns of Bethlehem.

I think after what Murray said you can disregard his testimony. He was a clear liar on the stand. He did a lot of things they wanted him to do. He wanted people to say things that you could hear, that would make you think these demonstrators were violent people. He had some really rough ones in there. He had, "The Hump Sucks," "Daley Sucks the Hump"—pretty rough expressions. He didn't have "Peace Now." He didn't hear that. He didn't give you any others. Oh, I think he had "Charge. The street is ours. Let's go."

That is what he wanted you to hear. He was as accurate about that as he was about the Viet Cong flag, and remember his testimony about the whiffle balls. One injured his leg. Others he picked up. Where were those whiffle balls in this courtroom?

You know what a whiffle ball is. It is something you can hardly throw. Why didn't the Government let you see the whiffle ball? They didn't let you see it because it can't be thrown. They didn't let you see it because the nails are shiny. I got a glimpse of it. Why didn't you see it? They want you to see a photograph so you can see that the nails don't drop out on the photograph. We never saw any of these weapons. That is enough for Mr. Murray. I have, I think, wasted more time than he is worth on Mr. Murray.

Now, I have one witness to discuss with you who is extremely important and gets us into the alleged attack on the Grant Park underground garage.

This is the most serious plan that you have had. This is more serious than attacking the pigs, as they tried to pin onto the Yippies and the National Mobe. This is to bomb. This is frightening, this concept of bombing an underground garage, probably the most frightening concept that you can imagine.

By the way, Grant Park garage is impossible to bomb with Molotov cocktails. It is pure concrete garage. You won't find a stick of wood in it, if you go there. But, put that aside for the moment. In a mythical tale, it doesn't matter that buildings won't burn.

In judging the nonexistence of this so-called plot, you must remember the following things.

Lieutenant Healy in his vigil, supposedly, in the garage, never saw anything in anybody's hands, not in Shimabukuro's, whom he says he saw come into the garage, not in Lee Weiner's hands, whom he said he saw come into the garage, or any of the other four or five people whom he said he saw come into the garage. These people that he said he saw come into the garage were looking, he said, in two cars. What were they looking into cars for? You can ask that question. Does that testimony make any sense, that they come in empty-handed into a garage, these people who you are supposed to believe were going to fire bomb the underground garage?

Just keep that in mind when you consider this fairy tale when you are in the jury room.

Secondly, in considering it you have the testimony of Lieutenant Healy, who never saw Lee Wiener before. You remember he said "I never saw him before. I had looked at some pictures they had shown me."

But he never had seen him and he stands in a stairwell behind a closed door looking through a one-foot-by-one-foot opening in that door with chicken wire across it and a double layer of glass for three to four seconds, he said, and he could identify what he said was Lee Wiener in three to four seconds across what he said was thirty to forty yards away.

MR. FORAN: Your Honor, I object to "three or four seconds." It was five minutes.

MR. KUNSTLER: No, sir. The testimony reads, your Honor, that he identified him after three or four seconds and if Mr. Foran will look —

MR. FORAN: Then he looked at him for five minutes.

MR. KUNSTLER: He identified him after three or four seconds.

THE COURT: Do you have the transcript there?

MR. FORAN: Your Honor, I would accept that. He identified him immediately but he was looking at him for five minutes.

MR. KUNSTLER: I just think you ought to consider that in judging, Lieutenant Healy's question. This officer was not called before the grand jury investigating that very thing. And I think you can judge the importance of that man's testimony on whether he ever did tell the United States Attorney anything about this in September of 1968.

I submit he didn't because it didn't happen. It never happened. This is a simple fabrication. The simple truth of the matter is that there never was any such plot and you can prove it to yourselves. Nothing was ever found, there is no visible proof of this at all. No bottles. No rags. No sand. No gasoline. It was supposed to be a diversionary tactic, Mr. Schultz told you in his summation. This was a diversionary tactic. Diversionary to what? This was Thursday night.

If you will recall, the two marches to the Amphitheatre that got as far as 16th and 18th streets on Michigan had occurred earlier. The only thing that was left was the Downers Grove picnic. It was a diversionary operation to divert attention from the picnic at Downers Grove. It was diversionary to nothing. The incident lives only in conversations, the two conversations supposedly overheard by Frapolly and Bock, who are the undercover agents who were characterized, I thought, so aptly by Mr. Weinglass.

Now just a few more remarks. One, I want to tell you that as jurors, as I have already told you, you have a difficult task. But you also have the obligation if you believe that these seven men are not guilty to stand on that and it doesn't matter that other jurors feel the other way. If you honestly and truly believe it, you must stand and you must not compromise on that stand.

MR. FORAN: Your Honor, I object to that. Your Honor will instruct the jury what their obligations are.

THE COURT: I sustain the objection. You are getting into my part of the job.

MR. KUNSTLER: What you do in that jury room, no one can question you on. It is up to you. You don't have to answer as to it to anybody and you must stand firm if you believe either way and not —

MR. FORAN: Your Honor, I object to that.

THE COURT: I sustain the objection. I told you not to talk about that, Mr. Kunstler.

MR. KUNSTLER: I think I have a right to do it.

THE COURT: You haven't a right when the Court tells you not to and it is a matter of law that is peculiarly my function. You may not tell the jury what the law is.

MR. KUNSTLER: Before I come to my final conclusion, I want to thank you both for myself, for Mr. Weinglass, and for our clients for your attention. It has been an ordeal for you, I know. We are sorry that it had to be so. But we are grateful that you have listened. We know you will weigh, free of any prejudice on any level, because if you didn't, then the jury system would be destroyed and would have no meaning whatsoever. We are living in extremely troubled times, as Mr. Weinglass pointed out. An intolerable war abroad has divided and dismayed us all. Racism at home and poverty at home are both causes of despair and discouragement. In a so-called affluent society, we have people starving, and people who can't even begin to approximate the decent life.

These are rough problems, terrible problems, and as has been said by everybody in this country, they are so enormous that they stagger the imagination. But they don't go away by destroying their critics. They don't vanish by sending men to jail. They never did and they never will.

To use these problems by attempting to destroy those who protest against them is probably the most indecent thing that we can do. You can crucify a Jesus, you can poison a Socrates, you can hang John Brown or Nathan Hale, you can kill a Che Guevara, you can jail a Eugene Debs or a Bobby Seale. You can assassinate John Kennedy or a Martin Luther King, but the problems remain. The solutions are essentially made by continuing and perpetuating with every breath you have the right of men to think, the right of men to speak boldly and unafraid, the right to be masters of their souls, the right to live free and to die free. The hangman's rope never solved a single problem except that of one man.

I think if this case does nothing else, perhaps it will bring into focus that again we are in that moment of history when a courtroom becomes the proving ground of whether we do live free and whether we do die free. You are in that position now. Suddenly all importance has shifted to you—shifted to you as I guess in the last analysis it should go, and it is really your responsibility, I think, to see that men remain able to think, to speak boldly and unafraid, to be masters of their souls, and to live and die free. And perhaps if you do what is right, perhaps Allen Ginsberg will never have to write again as he did in "Howl," "I saw the best minds of my generation destroyed by madness," perhaps Judy Collins will never have to stand in any Courtroom again and say as she did, "When will they ever learn? When will they ever learn?"

# Defendant Statements And Sentencing

THE COURT: I now proceed with the imposition of sentence.

MR. KUNSTLER: Your Honor, we were not informed on Wednesday that sentence would occur today.

THE COURT: There is no obligation of a Court to notify you of every step it takes.

MR. KUNSTLER: Well, it is wrong, your Honor, both morally and I think legally.

THE COURT: If you are telling me I am morally wrong in this case, you might add to your difficulty. Be careful of your language, sir. I know you don't frighten very easily.

MR. KUNSTLER: The defendants had no way of knowing they are going to be sentenced today. Their families are not even present, which would seem to me in common decency would be permitted.

THE COURT: The reason they were kept out is my life was threatened by one of the members of the family. I was told they would dance on my grave in one of the hearings here within the last week.

MR. KUNSTLER:  Your Honor, are you serious?

THE COURT:  Yes, I am, sir.

MR. KUNSTLER:  Well, your Honor, I have no answer for that then.

THE COURT:  I am not a law enforcement officer.

MR. KUNSTLER:  It is your life.

THE COURT:  I deny your motion to defer sentencing.

MR. KUNSTLER:  I think my other applications, your Honor, can await sentencing.  I have several other applications.

THE COURT:  All right, I will hear from you first then with respect to the defendant David T. Dellinger.

MR. KUNSTLER:  Your Honor, I think for all of the defendants, Mr. Weinglass and I are going to make no statement.  The defendants will speak for themselves.

THE COURT:  All right, Mr. Dellinger, you have the right to speak in your own behalf.

MR. DELLINGER:  I would like to make four brief points.
First, I think that every judge should be required to spend time in prison before sentencing other people there so that he might become aware of the degrading antihuman conditions that persist not only in Cook County Jail but in the prisons generally of this country.  I feel more compassion for you, sir, than I do any hostility.  I feel that you are a man who has had too much power over the lives of too many people for too many years.  You are doing, and undoubtedly feeling correct and righteous, as often happens when people do the most abominable things.

My second point is whatever happens to us, however unjustified, will be slight compared to what has happened already to the Vietnamese people, to the black people in this country, to the criminals with whom we are now spending our days in the Cook County jail.  I must have already lived longer than the normal life expectancy of a black person born when I was born, or born now. I must have already lived longer, twenty years longer, than the normal life expectancy in the underdeveloped countries which this country is trying to profiteer from and keep under its domain and control.

Thirdly, I want to say that sending us to prison, any punishment the Government can impose upon us, will not solve the problem of this country rampant racism, will not solve the problem of economic injustice, it will not solve the problem of the foreign policy and the attacks upon the underdeveloped people of the world.

The Government has misread the times in which we live, just like there was a time when it was possible to keep young people, women, black people, Mexican-American, anti-war people, people who believe in truth and justice and really believe in democracy, which it is going to be possible to keep them quiet or suppress them.

Finally, all the way through this I have been ambivalent in my attitude toward you because there is something spunky about you that one has to admire, however misguided and intolerant I believe you are. All the way through the trial, sort of without consciousness or almost against my own will I keep comparing you to George III of England, perhaps because you are trying to hold back the tide of history although you will not succeed, perhaps because you are trying to stem and forestall a second American revolution.

I only wish that we were all not just more eloquent, I wish we were smarter, more dedicated, more united. I wish we could work together. I wish we could reach out to the Forans and the Schultzes and the Hoffmans, and convince them of the necessity of this revolution.

I think I shall sleep better and happier with a greater sense of fulfillment in whatever jails I am in for the next however many years than if I had compromised, if I had pretended the problems were any less real than they are, or if I had sat here passively in the courthouse while justice was being throttled and the truth was being denied. . . .

THE COURT: Mr. Davis, would you like to speak in your own behalf? You have that right.

MR. DAVIS: I do not think that it is a time to appeal to you or to appeal the system that is about to put me away. I think that what moves a government that increasingly is controlled by a police mentality is action. It is not a time for words; it is a time that demands action.

And since I did not get a jury of my peers, I look to the jury that is in the streets. My jury will be in the streets tomorrow all across the country and the verdict from my jury will keep coming for the next long five years that you are about to give me in prison.

When I come out of prison it will be to move next door to Tom Foran. I am going to be the boy next door to Tom Foran and the boy next door, the boy that could have been a judge, could have been a prosecutor, could have been a college professor, is going to move next door to organize his kids into the revolution. We are going to turn the sons and daughters of the ruling class in this country into Viet Cong.

THE COURT: Mr. Hayden, you have the right to speak in your own behalf.

MR. HAYDEN: I have very little that I want to say because I don't have very much respect for this kind of freedom of speech. This is the kind of freedom of speech that I think the Government now wants to restrict us to, freedom to speak in empty rooms in front of prosecutors, a few feet from your jail cell.

We have known all along what the intent of the Government has been. We knew that before we set foot in the streets of Chicago. We knew that before we set foot on the streets of Chicago. We knew that before the famous events of August 28, 1968. If those events didn't happen, the Government would have had to invent them as I think it did for much of its evidence in this case, but because they were bound to put us away.

They have failed. Oh, they are going to get rid of us, but they made us in the first place. We would hardly be notorious characters if they had left us alone in the streets of Chicago last year, but instead we became the architects, the masterminds, and the geniuses of a conspiracy to overthrow the government. We were invented. We were chosen by the Government to serve as scapegoats for all that they wanted to prevent happening in the 1970s.

I have sat there in the Cook County Jail with people who can't make bond, with people who have bum raps, with people who are nowhere, people who are the nothings of society, people who say to me, "You guys burned your draft cards. I would like to burn my birth certificate so they can never find me again."

I sit there and watch television, and I hear Mr. Foran say the system works, this trial proves the system works. Mr. Foran, I would love to see a television cameraman come into Cook County jail and show the people how the system is working. Maybe you could televise us sitting around the table with the roaches running over our wrists while we watch somebody on television, a constitutional expert explaining how the jury verdict demonstrates once again the vitality of the American system of justice.

If you didn't want to make us martyrs, why did you do it? If you wanted to keep it cool, why didn't you give us a permit? You know if you had given us a permit, you know that by doing this to us it speeds up the end for the people who do it to us.

And you know that if this prosecution had never been undertaken, it would have been better for those in power. It would have left them in power a little longer. You know that by doing this to us it speeds up the end for the people who do it to us.

You don't believe it but we have to do this. We have no choice. We had no choice in Chicago. We had no choice in this trial. The people always do what they have to do. Every person who is born now and every person under thirty now feels an imperative to do the kind of things that we are doing. They may not act on them immediately, but they feel the same imperative from the streets. Some day they are going to proclaim that imperative from the bench and from the courthouse. It's only a matter of time. You can give us time. You are going to give us time. But it is only a matter of time.

THE COURT: Mr. Hoffman, the law gives you the right to speak in your own behalf. I will hear from you if you have anything to say.

MR. HOFFMAN: Thank you. I feel like I have spent fifteen years watching John Daly shows about history. *You Are There.* It is sort of like taking LSD, which I recommend to you, Judge. I know a good dealer in Florida. I could fix you up.

Mr. Foran says that we are evil men, and I suppose that is sort of a compliment. He says that we are unpatriotic? I don't know, that has kind of a jingoistic ring. I suppose I am not patriotic.

But he says we are un-American. I don't feel un-American. I feel very American. I said it is not that the Yippies hate America. It is that they feel that the American Dream has been betrayed. That has been my attitude.

I know those guys on the wall. I know them better than you, I feel. I know Adams. I mean, I know all the Adams. They grew up twenty miles from my home in Massachusetts. I played with Sam Adams on the Concord Bridge. I was there when Paul Revere rode right up on his motorcycle and said, "The pigs are coming, the pigs are coming. Right into Lexington." I was there. I know the Adams. Sam Adams was an evil man.

Thomas Jefferson. Thomas Jefferson called for a revolution every ten years. Thomas Jefferson had an agrarian reform program that made Mao Tse Tung look like a liberal. I know Thomas Jefferson.

Hamilton: Well, I didn't dig the Federalists. Maybe he deserved to have his brains blown out.

Washington? Washington grew pot. He called it hemp. It was called hemp them. He probably was a pot head.

Abraham Lincoln? There is another one. In 1861 Abraham Lincoln in his inaugural address said, and I quote "When the people shall grow weary of their constitutional right to amend the government, they shall exert their revolutionary right to dismember and overthrow that government."

If Abraham Lincoln had given that speech in Lincoln Park, he would be on trial right here in this courtroom, because that is an inciteful speech. That is a speech intended to create a riot.

I don't even know what a riot is. I thought a riot was fun. Riot means you laugh, ha, ha. That is a riot. They call it a riot.

I didn't want to be that serious. I was supposed to be funny. I tried to be, I mean, but it was sad last night. I am not made to be a martyr. I tried to sign up a few years, but I went down there. They ran out of nails. What was I going to do? So I ended up being funny.

It wasn't funny last night sitting in a prison cell, a 5 x 8 room, with not light in the room. I could have written a whole book last night. Nothing. No light in the room. Bedbugs all over. They bite. I haven't eaten in six days. I'm not on a hunger strike; you can call it that. It's just that the food stinks and I can't take it.

Well, we said it was like Alice in Wonderland coming in, now I feel like Alice in 1984, because I have lived through the winter of injustice in this trial.

And it's fitting that if you went to the South and fought for voter registration and got arrested and beaten eleven or twelve times on those dusty roads for no bread, it's only fitting that you be arrested and tried under the civil rights act. That's the way it works.

Just want to say one more thing. People—I guess that is what we are charged with—when they decide to go from one state of mind to another state of mind, when they decide to fly that route, I hope they go youth fare no matter what their age.

I will see you in Florida, Julie.

THE COURT: The next defendant, Mr. Rubin, do you desire to speak in your own behalf? You have that privilege.

MR. RUBIN: Well, five months are over. Look at the courtroom, fluorescent lighting. We sat for five months in swivel chairs. The press, the marshals, the judge, now it is over.

This is one of the proudest moments of my life. This one of the happiest moments of my life, if you can dig what I mean. I am happy because I am in touch with myself, because I know who I am. I am happy because I am associated with Rennie, Tom, Dave, Abby and myself. That makes me very happy.

This is my life. I used to look like this. I use to look like this, Judge. See? (*displaying picture*)

I was a reporter for a newspaper. Most everybody around this table once looked like this, and we all believed in the American system, believed in the court system, believed in the election system, believed that the country had some things wrong with it, and we tried to change it.

I'm being sentenced to five years not for what I did in Chicago—I did nothing in Chicago. I am going to jail because I am part of a historical movement and because of my life, the things I am trying to do, because, as Abbie said, we don't want to be—we don't want to have a piece of the pie.

We don't just want to be part of the American way of life. We don't want to live in the suburbs. We don't want to have college degrees. We don't want to stand before the judge and say, "Yes, we respect you judge, no matter what happens." We don't want that. We are moved by something else. We are moved by a firm belief in ourselves.

And you are sentencing us for being ourselves. That's our crime: being ourselves. Because we don't look like this anymore. That's our crime.

Judge, I want to give you a copy of my book. I want you to read it on your vacation in Florida, because this is why I am on trial. I inscribed it. I made two little inscriptions. One says, "Dear Julius, the demonstrations in Chicago in 1968 were the first steps in the revolution. What happened in the courtroom is the second step." Then I decided to add another note, and that was: "Julius, You radicalized more young people than we ever could. You're the country's top Yippie." I hope you will take it and read it.

What you are doing out there is creating millions of revolutionaries. Julius Hoffman, you have done more to destroy the court system in this country than any of us could have done. All we did was go to Chicago and the police system exposed itself as totalitarian.

And I am glad we exposed the court system because in millions of courthouses across this country blacks are being shuttled from the streets to the jails and nobody knows about it. They are forgotten men. There ain't a whole corps of press people sitting and watching. They don't care. You see what we have done is, we have exposed that. Maybe now people will be interested in what happens in the courthouse down the street because of what happened here. Maybe now people will be interested.

This is the happiest moment of my life.

THE DEFENDANTS: Right on.

THE COURT: I call on the Government to reply to the remarks of the defendants and each of them.

MR. FORAN: The Government has no comment on their remarks, your Honor, I think the evidence in this case speaks for itself.

THE COURT: Mr. Clerk, the defendant David T. Dellinger will be committed to the custody of the Attorney General of the United States or his authorized representative for imprisonment for a term of five years. Further, the defendant Dellinger will be fined the sum of $5,000 and costs of prosecution, the defendant to stand committed until the fine and costs have been paid. That sentence of five years will be concurrent with the sentence the court imposed for contempt of court previously. The two sentences will run concurrently.

Mr. Clerk, the defendant Rennard C. Davis will be committed to the custody of the Attorney General of the United States for a term of five years. Further a fine of—a fine will be imposed against Mr. Davis in the sum of $5,000 and costs of prosecution.

The defendant Thomas C. Hayden will be committed to the custody of the Attorney General of the United States for a term of five years. Further a fine of $5,000 and costs of prosecution will be imposed.

The defendant Abbott H. Hoffman will be committed to the custody of the Attorney General of the United States for imprisonment for a term of five years. Further a fine of $5,000 and costs—

MR. HOFFMAN: Five thousand dollars, Judge? Could you make that three-fifty?

THE COURT: —$5,000 and—

MR. HOFFMAN: How about three and a half?

THE COURT: —and costs will be imposed, costs of prosecution will be imposed.

The defendant Jerry C. Rubin will be committed to the custody of the Attorney General of the United States for a term of five years. Further there will be a fine of $5,000 and cost of prosecution will be imposed.

Not only on the record in this case, covering a period of four months or longer, but from the defendants made here today, the

Court finds that the defendants are clearly dangerous persons to be at large. Therefore the commitments here will be without bail.

THE COURT: Does the defense have any observations?

MR. KUNSTLER: In conclusion, your Honor, speaking both for Mr. Weinglass and myself, we didn't need to hear our clients speak today to understand how much they meant to us but, after listening to them a few moments ago we know that what they have said here has more meaning and will be longer remembered than any words said by us or by you.

We feel that if you could even begin to understand that simple fact, then their triumph would have been as overwhelming today as is our belief—

MR. KUNSTLER: —as inevitable—

THE COURT: I gave you an opportunity to speak at the very beginning. You said counsel did not desire to speak.

MR. KUNSTLER: Your Honor, couldn't I say my last words without you cutting me off?

THE COURT: You said you didn't want to speak.

MR. KUNSTLER: Your Honor, I just said a moment ago we had a concluding remark. Your Honor has succeeded perhaps, in sullying it, and I think maybe that is the way the case should end, as it began.

ABBIE HOFFMAN: We love our lawyers.

THE COURT: Mr. Marshal, the court will be in recess.

Vergne, TN USA
nuary 2011
?5LV00006B/145/P

9 781934 941355